C000050905

the **CHARA**
of **FASHION**

MULTI TALENTED GOD

This is very much a collaborative book. First thanks, therefore, are to all those who have contributed - for most it was a process of agreeing to take part (!), meeting up, reviewing my take on what we had discussed, and then feeding back thoughts - no small commitment of time and effort. Thank you.

Katrina Lawson Johnston has supplied many images throughout the book. Thank you. Katrina's story is included in the Ten Stories of Faith section.

With thanks to all the models, and their agencies, where I have included images taken myself at shows - included because I think you look great - and with particular apologies if you are startled to see yourself in the context of this book.

Thank you to Debbie Clinton, the Diocese of London's Capital Vision Manager, and Rev Peterson Feital, who helped make many initial connections.

Thank you to the many people working in the fashion industry - with whom I have shared an inspiring, if sometimes challenging, thirty-seven year walk.

And to my wife, Gill, who shares my every days, and has to live with my frequent and long absences upstairs in the study.

Simon Ward
July 2016

wb

published by *white*bench
www.multitalentedgod.com
www.simonwardlondon.com
copyright © Simon Ward 2016

All rights reserved. No part of this publication may be reproduced, stored in a retrieval system, or transmitted in any form or by any means, electronic, mechanical, photocopying or otherwise, without the prior written consent of the publisher. Short extracts may be used for review purposes.

Unless othwerwise noted, Scripture quotations from the Holy Bible, New International Version Anglicised, NIV Copyright © 1979, 1984, 2011 by Biblica, Inc Used by permission. All rights reserved worldwide.

ISBN 978-0-993247-82-8
Printed in Malta by Progress Press Co. Ltd

CONTENTS 1

CONTENTS 2

fashion images: the author's own, except where credited

FOREWORDS

RT REV ROB WICKHAM, BISHOP OF EDMONTON
Sponsor, Diocese of London, Capital Vision 2020 Ambassadors

CAPITAL VISION 2020 is an initiative of the Diocese of London, seeking to equip Christians who are living and working in London to be more confident in speaking and living the Gospel of Jesus Christ, more compassionate in serving communities with the love of God the Father, and more creative in reaching new people and places in the power of the Spirit.

Simon's book is a valuable new tool to help Christians, including our Capital Vision 2020 Ambassadors, as they work through the practicalities of implementing these goals in the challenging everyday world of the 21st Century. The fashion world speaks of enormous creativity, as does God's story. This book tells some of those stories, which will provide a rich and varied insight for those whose career is already in fashion and those aspiring to follow in their footsteps. Whatever our day job, I pray that we can all learn from our shared stories.

RT REV ADRIAN NEWMAN, BISHOP OF STEPNEY
Sponsor, Diocese of London, Creative Network

CREATIVITY stands at the heart of communication. The Character of Fashion takes an intruiging and highly creative perspective on a world that is at the same time mysterious to the outsider, and yet engaged in, at least to some extent, by all of us as consumers. Simon's career, at the highest level of the fashion industry, combined with his gifts as an astute observer, insightful thinker and accessible writer, along with his passion to see the transforming power of Jesus at work in contemporary society, makes him uniquely placed to lift the lid on this great, but challenging industry. Simon's core question "If God was boss, how might He run fashion?" is the perfect starting point for an insightful and stimulating assessment, concluding in the thought provoking, but entirely logical idea that an industry has a character, and that character is determined, and can be changed, both by those working in it and the decisions taken by its consumers.

PROFESSOR FRANCES CORNER OBE
Head, London College of Fashion,
Pro Vice-Chancellor, University of the Arts London

THE CHARACTER OF FASHION is a fascinating and
original interpretation of the world of fashion. Simon asks
what fashion would be like if God were in charge, and his
exploration of this question, with insight from many different
members of the fashion community, is enlightening and
thought-provoking. Simon's career at the helm of British
fashion, combined with his commitment to faith, provides
a really unique perspective. He explores many of the
environmental and social issues fashion is faced with,
and provides a framework for addressing them. The
book makes all of us involved in fashion consider how
we can make our industry a better place to work in.

DYLAN JONES OBE, Editor, British GQ

THE CHARACTER OF FASHION is an ambitious project, seeking to
lift the lid, for those looking in, on some of the issues that make fashion the
extraordinary, yet complex industry that it is; and then, through the lens of the
author's faith, shining a light on it in a way that doesn't preach, but invites all of
us who make our living in fashion, to consider how its considerable heft might
be used to help make the world a better place. No bad thing. I think Simon has
got the balance right and this book is a worthwhile addition to the reading list
of anyone interested in what makes fashion tick.

AUTHOR'S COMMENT ON METHODOLOGY

*THIS is the first in a series of explorations into a variety of industries and
sectors. It attempts to tread a fine line, presenting the views and input of
Christians, alongside those who do not share that faith.*

*I have sought to make it clear where I am talking to experts in their field,
regardless of faith, and where I talk to Christians to explore how God might look
at fashion. I hope it is obvious - sections 2, 4, 6 & 7 look through a 'Christian' lens,
section 5 & 8 largely focus on the views as seen from the industry, and sections
3, 8 & 9 incorporate something of both, including many of my own perspectives.*

*I hope the result does justice to and respects the views of all those who have
been so kind with their time and input - regardless of the fact that, in all
probability, not all will agree with everything said.*

GOD IS A
FASHION DESIGNER!

INTRODUCTION

MULTI TALENTED GOD
- AN INTRODUCTION

making a difference at work

MULTI TALENTED GOD?

"GOD IS A FASHION DESIGNER!" So ran the headline above an online review, the day after an event at which I spoke about "A life of faith in the world of fashion." It was forwarded to me by my PR department at the British Fashion Council, who picked it up - "Great review, Simon!"

A friend, working in construction, who had been at the event, also saw the review and emailed me that afternoon: "Heh, God is a civil engineer as well!"

The seed was sewn ... oops, sown! The Creator is a Multi talented God, not just interested in those working in all manner of different jobs, but passionate about the work itself and the way it is carried out. The Bible speaks into our world of work and our own stories bring alive the principles laid out millenia ago.

Scroll back a couple of years ... I was helping a great fashion friend of mine, Chrissie Abbott, as she got Fashion for Christ up and running. FFC is a support group for those working in fashion, and we were having a prayer room for the first time the following weekend in Somerset House, at the heart of London Fashion Week. I was pondering what we might pray about - something a bit more insightful than: "Please make the shows a success and help everyone write lots of orders."

I started jotting down a few thoughts as to what might be God's priorities if He was in charge. It was big picture stuff and, when I finished, I ran my finger down the list. There were ten items. I laughed out loud, it was obvious; here were ... GOD'S TEN COMMANDMENTS FOR FASHION.

MULTI TALENTED GOD does not give advice on how to evangelise work colleagues! Rather, it explores where and how God might already be at work in what we all do day by day. My hope and prayer is that MULTI TALENTED GOD will not just inspire Christians to see how they can be making a difference at work; it will also equip them with a new confidence and vocabulary to bring salt and light to their every day lives, unleashing fresh engagement with those they spend the majority of their waking lives with, regardless of where they stand on faith.

FRESH PERSPECTIVE ON FAITH & THE WORKPLACE

A NOTE TO THE CHURCHES

35 YEARS working in fashion as a Christian have revealed a number of things:

- there are many great people working in fashion, but there are also those trapped by the (false) notion that fashion is the most important thing in the world;
- fashion is not an easy place to talk openly about the Christian faith and I have singularly failed to 'evangelise' my fellow workers;
- if this was crucial, I would be right in feeling very guilty;
- God, however, has shown favour to me in enabling me to have a 'successful' career, even though I have often questioned if it was the right place for me;
- this implies to me that God has wanted me to learn from the world of fashion;
- it is crucial that Christians act as salt and light in a spiritually high risk industry;
- a fresh approach may be appropriate to reveal God's love for a needy world.

Reflecting on this over a number of years, has led me to the following conclusion:

- Christianity has a poor reputation in the average 21st Century Western workplace;
- traditional 'evangelism' may not be the most effective way to share God's love;
- if there was an alternative, it might release millions of Christians from feeling guilt at their own ineffectiveness and set them free to help change the world;
- all Christians are called to be salt and light to prevent decay, bring out flavour and reveal things as they really are;
- a serious focus should be placed on how to be this salt and light, in a way that is relevant to the jobs we do and the people we work with, because ...
- work is the place, and these are the people with whom we spend most time, engage with life's challenges and who see what we are really like and what we stand for.

Rather than focussing so much resource trying to bring people into church, should not churches be empowering people in their day to day work? For:

- I am the vicar in my workplace
- my workplace is my parish
- my industry is my diocese

MULTI TALENTED GOD tries to define and resource such a fresh approach.

WHO IS MULTI TALENTED GOD WRITTEN FOR?

MULTI TALENTED GOD seeks to engage with three groups:

1. CHRISTIANS WORKING IN FASHION

ENDORSING the fact that fashion is an important industry for Christians to work in

EDUCATING them as to the big issues and how God would wish them to be approached

EMPOWERING them to approach their day to day work from a distinct and Godly point of view

2. THE CHURCH

INFORMING church leaders and members about the world of fashion with all its opportunities and challenges

INVOLVING them with their colleagues in fashion, particularly through praying for them and others who work in the industry

INSPIRING them as consumers to make considered choices that they, too, may have a story to tell

3. EVERYONE

CHAMPIONING good practice that will help make the world a better place

CHALLENGING negative views of Christians

CHANGING the idea that Christianity has no relevance to the everyday world of work

opposite:
PUTTING COMPASSION INTO FASHION
Compassion UK fashion show, April 2015

A VERY DIFFERENT
SET OF PRIORITIES

OVERVIEW

THE CHARACTER OF FASHION - AN OVERVIEW

if God was in charge of fashion ...

IF GOD WAS IN CHARGE OF FASHION
I HAVE NO DOUBT HE WOULD HAVE SOME
VERY DIFFERENT PRIORITIES TO THOSE GOVERNING
MUCH THAT GOES ON IN THE INDUSTRY TODAY.
NEVERTHELESS, THERE IS A GREAT DEAL THAT GOD
WOULD SURELY WISH TO ENDORSE AND APPLAUD.
LET'S START THERE.

DESIGN, clothing, fashion ... they are strewn through the Bible: from the act of Creation to Adam and Eve's first wardrobe; from the design of the tabernacle to the first priestly robes; from multiple imagery illustrating key principles underlying the life of faith, to the radiant garments clothing Christ in glory. Any suggestion that God and fashion simply don't mix seems entirely off the mark.

In fact, quite the opposite: I would be so bold as to suggest that God loves fashion, with all the complexities surrounding it. And, yes, I think He revels in the challenges fashion throws up, as they test our ability to combine individual creativity with team-work to achieve goals that can transform the lives of millions across the globe ... with benefit to all, if we can get it right.

The stories shared in this book reveal that there are many paths leading into fashion, and this is reflected in the rich diversity of talented people involved. Forget the lazy stereotype of an industry inhabited solely by champagne luvvies and social media addicts who spend their entire lives swapping notes on the latest micro trend, unconcerned by how the rest of the world may be affected.

There are a great many involved in the world of fashion who recognise, full well, that fashion isn't everything, yet pour their best efforts into creating and selling clothes that can focus and convey identity, enhance individuality and help bring out inner beauty.

Is it an industry I would recommend to a youngster looking for a vibrant and challenging career? Absolutely. There is much opportunity for those who are prepared to give it their best shot.

And as consumers we can be involved - *are* involved - through our purchasing decisions. We are all part of fashion.

Yet ... speaking to a wide range of people working in and around the industry, along with my own thirty-five years' experience, it is clear there are many ways that things are done which fall foul of what I believe to be God's underlying heart for all human activity:

What does the Lord require of you? to act justly, love mercy and walk humbly with your God. Micah 6:8

Love your neighbour as yourself Matthew 22:39

THE THING GOD MIGHT BE MOST CONCERNED ABOUT IS THE CHARACTER OF THE INDUSTRY AND THOSE INVOLVED WITH IT, AS EMPLOYEES AND CONSUMERS

THE idea that consumers can enjoy endless cheap clothes, without it impacting the livelihoods of those working along the supply chain, and around the planet we share, is ridiculous. Where's the justice there?

The idea that stylists creating looks for the catwalks and magazines, which idealise looks completely unobtainable by the vast majority of the massive audiences they reach, is irresponsibility on an industrial scale. Where's the mercy in that?

The idea that fashion might somehow be unreachable for the average Joe, drawing purely from the educated or privileged, is folly. Anyone heard of humility?

The idea that people can be used as human fodder to work all hours, often without pay, or be spat out, is as insulting as it is short-sighted. How does that display love for my neighbour?

There is much that is good and great in fashion, and that must be celebrated. However, behind much of that which is wrong lie two false gods: money and self.

Fast fashion, sweat-shop labour, unpaid internships, unsustainable use of the planet's resources, the sexualisation (through age inappropriate clothing) of children, unhealthy body images, drivenness and extended long hours, disdain for those outside the 'in crowd' … all these have their roots in an uncaring accumulation of wealth and disregard for others' welfare and opportunity.

Unsurprising that many would consider fashion to be a brutal, exploitative and narcissistic industry.

This book does not seek to sort out all these issues, although it explores a number of them.

What it does is to conclude that the thing God might be most concerned about is the character of the industry and those involved with it, as employees and consumers.

It also suggests that Christians, standing alongside all those, regardless of faith, who care about our fellow occupants of this precious planet, should be at the forefront, working tirelessly to see that justice and mercy prevail over greed and exploitation.

FASHION MATTERS. TO THE
ECONOMY, TO SOCIETY AND
TO EACH OF US PERSONALLY.
FASTER THAN ANYTHING ELSE,
WHAT WE WEAR TELLS THE
STORY OF WHO WE ARE
OR WHO WE WANT TO BE

Professor Frances Corner OBE
Head, London College of Fashion

FASHION INSIGHT

INSIGHTS TO THE WORLD OF FASHION

fashion is not unlike marmite
... loved by some, loathed by others

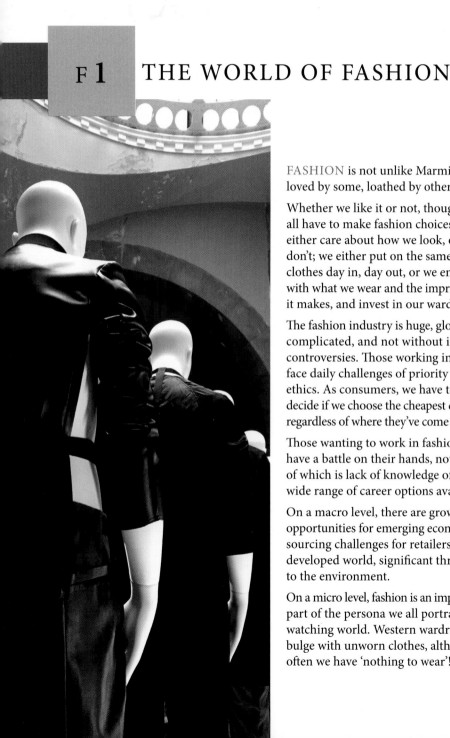

F **1** THE WORLD OF FASHION

FASHION is not unlike Marmite - loved by some, loathed by others!

Whether we like it or not, though, we all have to make fashion choices: we either care about how we look, or we don't; we either put on the same old clothes day in, day out, or we engage with what we wear and the impression it makes, and invest in our wardrobe.

The fashion industry is huge, global, complicated, and not without its controversies. Those working in it face daily challenges of priority and ethics. As consumers, we have to decide if we choose the cheapest clothes regardless of where they've come from.

Those wanting to work in fashion can have a battle on their hands, not least of which is lack of knowledge of the wide range of career options available.

On a macro level, there are growth opportunities for emerging economies, sourcing challenges for retailers in the developed world, significant threats to the environment.

On a micro level, fashion is an important part of the persona we all portray to a watching world. Western wardrobes bulge with unworn clothes, although often we have 'nothing to wear'!

THE images sent out by the fashion industry are hugely influential on young people, with the potential to impact eating disorders and create shopaholics.

The demands of the fashion cycle make huge demands on those working in it.

Standing back from all this, one cannot help but ask "is it all worth it?" How important is fashion, compared, for example, with health, education, housing, politics?

On one level, no, it's not so important. We could get by with a pair of jeans and a t-shirt and be done with it, without all the fuss.

Yet, the natural world around us points to something more beautiful, with more glorious potential than just the bare minimum. The creativity bestowed in men and women cries out for a greater ambition, without which the soul would wither and die.

We clothe ourselves for necessity, but we express ourselves with fashion.

This book lifts a corner of the veil that covers the world of fashion, giving a sneak preview, no more, into what it is, who makes it tick, the challenges it faces, and how God might see it.

TEN FASHION FACTS & FIGURES

IN 2010, the global clothing and textile industry amounted to £1,645 trillion.

FASHION is the 15th biggest industry in the UK, contributing £26 billion to the UK economy and employing 800,000 people.

THE CHINESE TEXTILE INDUSTRY CREATES 3 BILLION TONS OF SOOT EACH YEAR

£43 BILLION is spent on clothing each year by UK consumers.

OVER a lifetime, an American woman will spend $125,000 on clothes, including 271 pairs of shoes, 185 dresses and 145 bags.

A SINGLE TEXTILE MILL CAN USE 200 TONS OF WATER FOR EACH TON OF FABRIC DYED; MANY RIVERS RUN THE COLOURS OF THE SEASON, AS THE UNTREATED TOXIC DYES WASH OFF FROM MILLS

WOMEN'S nominal clothing sizes have increased in physical size over the years in a phenomenon known as "vanity sizing." A size 8 dress with a 32-inch bust in 1967 is now considered a size 0 today.

PINK used to be a colour primarily for men.

CHILDREN dressed identically to adults until the mid-1800s, when the concept of children's clothing took off.

2 BILLION t-shirts are sold each year.

THE PRICE OF CLOTHING HAS DECREASED BY 8.5% SINCE 1992, EVEN WHEN ADJUSTED FOR INFLATION

'JEANS' comes from the cotton trousers worn by 'Genes', the local term for Genoan sailors.

GLOBAL apparel business is expected to generate double digit growth between 2014 and 2020, much of it coming from developing markets.

PINK USED TO BE A COLOUR
PRIMARILY FOR MEN

15

TEN FASHION QUOTES

WHAT YOU WEAR IS HOW
YOU PRESENT YOURSELF
TO THE WORLD ...
ESPECIALLY TODAY, WHEN
HUMAN CONTACTS ARE
SO QUICK, FASHION IS
INSTANT LANGUAGE
Miuccia Prada

I FIRMLY BELIEVE THAT
WITH THE RIGHT
FOOTWEAR ONE CAN
RULE THE WORLD
Bette Midler

DEMAND QUALITY, NOT JUST
IN THE PRODUCT YOU BUY,
BUT IN THE LIFE OF THE
PERSON WHO MADE IT
Livia Firth

FASHION IS WHAT YOU'RE
OFFERED FOUR TIMES
A YEAR BY DESIGNERS.
STYLE IS WHAT YOU CHOOSE
Lauren Hutton

FASHION SHOULD BE A FORM
OF ESCAPISM AND NOT A
FORM OF IMPRISONMENT
Alexander McQueen

FASHIONS FADE
STYLE IS ETERNAL
Yves Saint-Laurent

ELEGANCE IS NOT
STANDING OUT BUT
BEING REMEMBERED
Giorgio Armani

STYLE IS A WAY TO SAY
WHO YOU ARE WITHOUT
HAVING TO SPEAK
Rachel Zoe

FASHION IS ABOUT SO MUCH
MORE THAN THE CLOTHES
WE WEAR. IT MAY BE AN
EXPRESSION OF OUR
PROFESSIONAL AND
PERSONAL IDENTITIES,
AN EXPRESSION OF WHERE
AND HOW WE SEE OURSELVES
IN RELATION TO OUR PEER
GROUP, OUR CULTURES, OUR
FAMILIES AND COMMUNITIES,
AN EXPRESSION OF OUR
CREATIVITY, OUR SENSE OF FUN
Baroness Lola Young, Co-chair
All-Party Parliamentary Group on
Ethics and Sustainability in Fashion

FASHION IS THE ARMOUR
TO SURVIVE THE REALITY
OF EVERYDAY LIFE
Bill Cunningham

IT COSTS A LOT OF MONEY
TO LOOK THIS CHEAP
Dolly Parton

A serious attempt to explain fashion
would be a book in its own right.
This selection of quotes, from those
who should know, will give a flavour.
nb. fashion folk do humour

A MAN SHOULD LOOK
AS IF HE HAS BOUGHT HIS
CLOTHES WITH INTELLIGENCE
PUT THEM ON WITH CARE
AND THEN FORGOTTEN
ALL ABOUT THEM
Hardy Amies

THE BEAUTY OF A WOMAN
IS NOT IN THE CLOTHES
SHE WEARS, THE FIGURE
THAT SHE CARRIES, OR THE
WAY SHE COMBS HER HAIR.
THE BEAUTY OF A WOMAN IS
SEEN IN HER EYES, BECAUSE
THAT IS THE DOORWAY
TO HER HEART
Audrey Hepburn

F 4   BRITISH MENSWEAR STEPS UP

DYLAN JONES SHARES 10 INSIGHTS

FASHION has become one of the iconic strands of modern British life. And not only do we excel at creating it, we've also become rather adept at exporting it.

London Collections Men, which I chair, was started as a platform for British designers, and has now grown to include international designers from all corners of the globe, from Europe and Asia to the US and beyond. The extraordinarily hard work of the British Fashion Council makes all this possible.

Menswear has become as important as womenswear in the last ten to fifteen years, in terms of its appeal to consumers, its ability to generate press attention and its profile on our high streets. Men are far more sophisticated consumers than they used to be, almost as sophisticated as women!

LCM has been built on the patronage of our supporters, not least our amazing ambassadors. These include David Gandy, Lewis Hamilton, Tinie Tempah, Nick Grimshaw, Dermot O'Leary and Chinese superstar Hu Bing. Each represents a vibrant part of the fashion, sports or entertainment industries.

Fashion is the largest employer of all the UK's creative industries. The sector also provides opportunities to minority groups to a greater extent than most other creative industries.

When we started London Collections Men, one of our aims was to host some of the very best dinners, cocktail parties and events in the calendar, thus ensuring that buyers and journalists turned up in Milan with the best hangovers money can buy.

Dylan Jones OBE is a British journalist and author who has served as editor of the UK version of men's fashion and lifestyle magazine GQ since 1999. He has held senior roles with several other publications, including editor of magazines i-D and Arena, and has contributed weekly columns to newspapers The Independent and The Mail on Sunday. Dylan has penned multiple books. Dylan is chairman of London Collections Men.

London is the centre of the fashion universe. Fact.
If you don't believe me, just look on Wikipedia.

If you're leaving a room full of more than four women,
try not to kiss the first one, as you'll be there all day.

On no account wear your sunglasses after dark.
Only Jack Nicholson can ever do this.

Baggy surfing shorts are just about OK, although I'd
rather you had IRONIC stencilled on your forehead.

Don't have IRONIC stencilled on your forehead,
or indeed anywhere else.

F 5   WHAT IS FASHION?

IS IT A CRIME TO LOVE FASHION?

FASHION has a way of polarising opinion ... as I was reminded when confronted by the message on a dress at London Fashion Week: *'If loving fashion is a crime, we are guilty'?* Love ... crime ... guilty? Strong words for what we wear!

Under 'Fashion's Big Issues', we take a look at 10 challenges faced by the industry. Here are some (intentionally provocative) opposites, as we consider what is fashion?

WORLDWIDE employer of millions ... or cesspit of sweatshop exploitation?

HOPELESS waste of space ... or joyful celebration of who we are?

ADDICTIVE hell ... or recreational heaven?

TEMPTING mistress ... or faithful friend?

IMPORTANT economic driver ... or destroyer of the planet?

SEASONAL inspiration ... or relentless hamster wheel?

FRIVOLOUS vanity ... or expression of confidence?

ALLURING party dress ... or invitation to abuse?

SLAVE driver ... or passionate pursuit?

HEDONISTIC hothouse ... or creative crucible?

INSIGHT to our personality ... or coat of protective armour?

OPPORTUNITY for invaluable experience ... or unpaid exploitation?

NOTHING to wear ... or wardrobe of delights?

In my experience, not unexpectedly, those who work in or follow fashion will tend to take the positive view, whereas those outside these camps may be inclined to think the worst of something they may not understand.

I will shortly suggest that God loves fashion and all those that work in it, even though some of its practices are well off the mark. If we want to look at fashion seriously, I guess we need to grapple with each issue and accept that a true assessment will include elements of both extremes set out above.

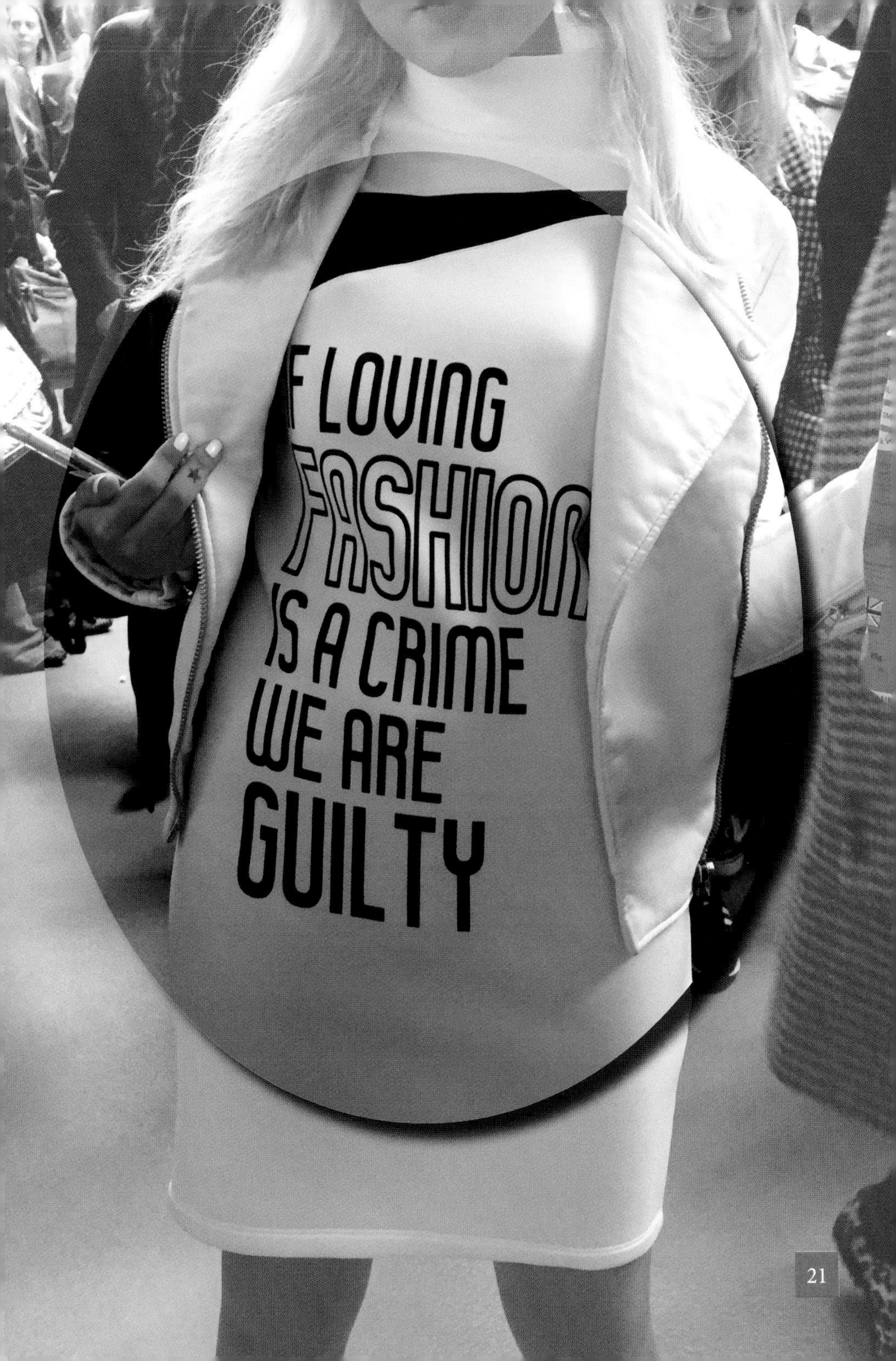
F LOVING
FASHIO
S A CRIME
WE ARE
GUILTY

ZOWIE BROACH'S TOP 10

CREATIVITY *Where does it come from?*
The truth here is that creativity is essential to our culture,
even our civilization, and we do not need to
explain everything to within an inch of its life …
some things we need to believe, without knowing.

RESEARCH *How much is inspiration, how much research?*
Ideas are not owned by us, we are possessed by them.

Zowie Broach
image: Maxyme G Delisle

ENTERTAINMENT *Should fashion be enjoyable?*
If you wish it to be… 'Fashion' is a personal response.

ART *How much fashion creativity is art, how much commerciality?*
This is wholly dependent on the individual designer or wearer.

TEN *Ten words that capture the essence of creativity?*
honesty truth danger exploration error explosion collision tenacity bravery attitude

IMITATION *Is any design original, or is it all imitation?*
Imitation is how we learn as a child … and then for the rest of our lives. This is not
to be misinterpreted as copy … this would be cheap and weak.

VALUES *How do a designer's values impact their creativity?*
Values make your manifesto of self; so they not only impact, they are what you
build upon, what you are about, what you breathe in.

IMPENETRABLE *Is it important that clothes are understood?*
No, not always. If we understood everything, we would not believe most of what
makes us who we are today. And no clothes lead us to understand gravity, as yet,
but never underestimate the power of self expression across time.

TWO *How important is partnership in creativity?*
Rarely do we live alone in our thoughts, without debate or conversation. Maybe we
need to do this more in fact. And so partnership is essential to find those you trust.
Equally we see, historically, the relationships that include creative and economic
thinking are almost always successful. NOTE - that both partners have creativity
in their methods and practise whether in design or finance.

YOU *Is creativity simply an expression of self?*
As Brian Eno declared in his John Peel Lecture: "art is everything we don't have to do."

HONESTY

TRUTH

DANGER

EXPLORATION

ERROR

EXPLOSION

COLLISION

TENACITY

BRAVERY

ATTITUDE

BOUDICCA

image: Chris Moore

Zowie Broach is Head of Fashion at the Royal College of Art. With Brian Kirkby, she founded the designer label BOUDICCA in 1997 as a purely artistic expression, showing in art galleries and other exhibition spaces. The brand has since garnered international plaudits for its visionary approach to fashion. A graduate of Plymouth (Fine Art) and Middlesex (Fashion Textiles), Zowie's 12 years as a fashion educator have included periods at the University of Westminster, Parsons in New York, SIAC in Chicago, and Bezalel Academy of Arts and Design, Jerusalem.

STAND FIRM ... WITH YOUR FEET
FITTED WITH THE READINESS THAT
COMES FROM THE GOSPEL OF PEACE
Ephesians 6:15

F 7 A BIBLE VIEW OF FASHION

A VERY BRIEF SUMMARY

IN THE BEGINNING ... God didn't draw up a business plan - He created the world ... and created it with outrageous variety - there are, for example, an estimated 100,000 species of tree. And - for those who tut-tut about the way fashions change so frequently - He created the seasons.

He was the first designer, dressing Adam and Eve, and a whole chapter *(Exodus 28)* is given over to the design of the first priestly garments. And there's some serious detail here: *"Fashion a breast-piece for making decisions - the work of a skilled craftsman. Make it like the ephod: of gold, and of blue, purple and scarlet yarn, and of finely twisted linen. It is to be square - a span long and a span wide - and folded double." Exodus 28:15,16*

The first believer in Europe was Lydia who, as we see in Acts 16, was a dealer in purple cloth.

Garments are used throughout the Bible as a picture of praise *(Isaiah 61)*, protection *(Ephesians 6)*, and change *(Ephesians 4: 22, 24)*.

But also a warning that our true beauty does not come from what we wear *(1 Peter 3)*.

The first insight we are given into what Jesus looks like in heaven is that he is: *dressed in a robe reaching down to his feet, with a golden sash around his chest. Revelation 1:14*

And then, in the glorious picture of the Holy City descending out of heaven, we are told that it is: *prepared as a bride, beautifully dressed for her husband Revelation 21:2 - more on this under: The Imagery of Clothes.*

It seems that fashion, clothing, textiles, design and creativity are woven into the very fabric of creation.

Their inclusion covers the practicalities of design and construction, the choice of fabric and accessories, the purpose of the garments made, and the imagery that they conjure up as a means of conveying a wide variety of truth.

Let's have a brief look at how this purpose and imagery give clothing a unique role in helping focus and portray identity and meaning.

FASHION, CLOTHING, TEXTILES, DESIGN AND CREATIVITY ARE WOVEN INTO THE VERY FABRIC OF CREATION

F 8   THE IMAGERY OF CLOTHES

CLOTHES pop up throughout the Bible as an image illustrating something greater than themselves - just as what we wear today can portray something greater about us than the way we look.

Here are some well known examples:

As God's chosen people, holy and dearly loved, clothe yourselves with compassion, kindness, humility, gentleness and patience Colossians 3:12

The apostle Paul (perhaps a surprising ambassador for fashion!), having argued that we are set free from historic rules and regulations through the perfect sacrifice of Jesus Christ, goes on to explain that our resultant freedom should not be used to indulge ourselves or exploit others; rather to live pure and beautiful lives. He lists some wonderful, Godly attributes and uses the imagery of putting them on as we would our clothes. He goes one step further in his letter to the church at Rome by stating that we are actually to clothe ourselves in Christ:

Clothe yourselves with the Lord Jesus Christ Romans 13:14

Just as our sinfulness is covered, like a garment, by the glorious perfection of Jesus, the clothing we wear doesn't just cover our nakedness; it can enhance and portray us in an altogether better light. If we take no care in our choice of clothes, simply throwing them on without a thought, we miss a great opportunity to communicate something of who we are.

I saw the Holy City, the new Jerusalem, coming down out of heaven from God, prepared as a bride beautifully dressed for her husband Revelation 21:2

I remember to this day the surge of pride as my wife appeared in a sunlit church door and started walking down the aisle. She looked so beautiful.

(nb. the image opposite is another bride!)

A wedding dress is meant to show off the bride at her best on her special day. The guests at the wedding dress up similarly to show respect for the bride, her husband and their families.

This sensitivity to what I wear and how it communicates to those I am with, plays out day to day. If I always wear the same jeans and t-shirt, I may feel relaxed, but it will be read differently by different people - some favourably, others less so.

A final image is clothing as armour ... protecting us. *Put on the full armour of God so that when the day of evil comes, you may be able to stand your ground Ephesians 6:13*

This can be looked at in two ways: literally, as a waterproof jacket will protect us against the elements. But also, a uniform will protect us with the reputation of the organisation. Conversely, we will swell with pride as we put on an England shirt (substitute your own favourite!) Like Paul's armour in Ephesians, some items are defensive, some help us go on the attack.

27

DURING the two
thousand or so fashion
shows I attended over
sixty-nine fashion weeks in London, I often found myself
sitting next to guests, from government ministers to
friends and family, who were unfamiliar with shows
and asked me just what was going on! I usually took them
on a imaginary guided tour of what was before them.
Here is a flavour of what they would have heard.

F 9
WHAT IS GOING ON AT A FASHION SHOW?
SIMON'S 10 POINT BRIEFING

VENUE is crucial - either for creating a unique environment or a simple backdrop to the clothes on show. And it has to be big enough to house reception areas, large backstage and the show space itself.

PR & SECURITY Fashion Week shows are by invitation only. The designer's PR company will invite you, welcome you, and try to find you a seat when yours has someone else in it. Security will do their best to make sure that the army of blaggers trying to get in (it's a part of most fashion courses!) are unsuccessful.

FRONT ROW Whilst the show is about the clothes and their designer, having a great front row adds a sense of occasion and anticipation - particularly when the paparazzi fly into a frenzy as celebs arrive.

PRESS & BUYERS On one side of the catwalk are the buyers - without them, a show is just an indulgence. On the other side are the press, who create the buzz around a designer and help them grow their business.

PHOTOGRAPHERS So much of fashion is about image. Without photographers, a show would just be a party for those in the room. With them, the show is wired around the world instantly. Good for publicity; not so good for design copyright! It's a hard job being a photographer, humping around great boxes of kit. But they're a hugely fun bunch of people.

LIGHTING is key - so images taken are up to an international standard. Hours are spent getting the lighting right and it is often the largest single show budget item.

HAIR & MAKE UP are dictated by the stylist who will create a mood for the way the collection is presented.

COLLECTION The clothes on show will be the fruit of months of research and development. The show will include show pieces, there just for press coverage.

MODELS bring the collection to life on the catwalk. Much ink is spilled on the size and shape of models. Much less on the crucial role they play in getting images used, and the calm demeanour they need to retain amongst the backstage storm that often rages around them.

AT THE HEART OF IT ALL IS THE DESIGNER. THE SHOW IS THE CULMINATION OF MONTHS OF HARD WORK

THE DESIGNER At the heart of it all is the designer. The show is the culmination of months of hard work, and so much depends on the response to their show. Not surprisingly, the only view the audience get is of a frazzled figure at the end of the show popping their head out for a few seconds before returning backstage for a round of exhausting interviews.

29

F 10 WHAT MIGHT JESUS WEAR TODAY?

10 WARDROBE SUGGESTIONS FOR THE 21ST CENTURY

A WHOLE CHAPTER in the Old Testament book of Exodus, chapter 28, is given over to what the Israelite priests should wear, and what the clothes symbolised.

Jesus was both priest and king, so we should read these words with some interest when considering what He might wear today. Yet, Jesus was also an everyday man, attending weddings, chatting to people on the streets, hiking long distances.

If He was so adaptable in the people He met, and the setting in which He met them, I think it would be quite wrong to assume that Jesus would wear just the 21st Century equivalent of the flowing robes and sandals of 1st Century Palestine that we imagine He wore then ... and nothing else. Surely He would dress, maybe not so much to impress, but to respect the people He engaged with and make them feel comfortable in His presence.

Back to Exodus chapter 28, there are many pointers to the clothing spec that God *(who dictated the requirements - see Exodus 25:1)* wanted for His representatives. Here are a few ideas that pick up on and adapt these to suggest a 21st Century take.

1. construction *(Exodus 28:3,7)* - the author of creation would want well made clothes
2. good materials *(28:5)* - a silk shirt (probably understated) for a king?
3. wording *(28:9-14)* - a slogan t-shirt with challenging message to those He met?
4. colours *(28:5)* - and many of them - Jesus was the agent of Creation with its endless variety and infinite shades of pattern and colour
5. a varied wardrobe *(28:4)* - Jesus would travel the world and need plenty of options
6. skilled craftsmen given wisdom by God *(28:3)* - to mix and match different items
7. purpose - to give dignity and honour *(28:2)* - Jesus would meet with leaders
8. to serve as priest, sacred garments *(28:3,4)* - Jesus would respect His church
9. shoes - crucial! *(Revelation 1:15)* - feet of burnished bronze
10. white - white is a widely recognised colour for purity and simplicity, but I wonder if Jesus might enjoy the jaunty take of this gentleman on a scooter ... which would help Him get around in an environmentally friendly fashion!

These wardrobe suggestions are presented with an substantial element of fun. Yet, the idea is an important one - the way we look says a lot about not just who we are, but how we want others to see and engage with us.

TEN 21st CENTURY
WARDROBE ITEMS
FOR JESUS

31

I DON'T DESIGN
CLOTHES
I DESIGN DREAMS

Ralph Lauren

STORIES

4

TEN STORIES OF FAITH IN THE WORLD OF FASHION

told as it is ... direct from fashion's front line

DANIEL BLAKE

image: Chris Brock

Daniel is a London-based fashion designer. For eleven years, he has run his own design business, for the first five years wholesaling the collection to independent retailers. He now sells direct to clients through twice yearly pop up events. He lectures two days a week at the London College of Fashion, teaching design and research on the bespoke tailoring course. Married to Clare, they have three young children.

WWW.DANIELBLAKE.CO.UK

IF YOU HAVE A DREAM
DON'T GIVE UP
DON'T LET CIRCUMSTANCES
PUT YOU OFF

EARLY YEARS

daniel's story

I wanted to be a fashion designer from as far back as I can remember. It's not entirely surprising - my mother was an interior designer and my step-dad was a textile designer.

Brought up in the remote south-west Wales countryside, there were not many of the usual distractions. At school, when other boys were kicking a ball around the playground at lunchtime, I was in the art room, drawing - I just loved the creative outlet it provided.

Rather than making me feel lonely, though, this stage of my life was like a crucible, where I could explore and develop my gifts.

My first outfit was a wedding dress made for my twelve year old sister, out of grandmother's old curtains.

A couple of years later, aged fourteen, a real wedding dress for my cousin was to be the catalyst that took me to London for a week's work experience in the studio of the dress designer, Helen Kent.

For a while, I had had a sense of needing to 'get to London' and this was the first tangible step on my journey to becoming a designer.

It was my first real experience of God's graciousness in making connections and opening up opportunities. Many more were to follow in the years ahead.

UNIVERSITY AND MY FIRST JOB

HAVING taken an additional arts subject at GCSE, I went on to a Foundation course in Plymouth, which helped me decide that I wanted to follow a fashion path rather than fine arts. This course was the most enjoyable year of the whole education process, with an opportunity to explore my creativity and build a portfolio. I would strongly recommend such a course to anyone considering a design career.

I then studied fashion design at Kingston University, benefitting from tuition by Ian Griffiths (now Creative Director at Max Mara) and Gordon Richardson (ditto at Topman). I loved the sense of competition with other like-minded people around me - it was a real incubator to germinate talent. Highlights were a factory visit to Italy and winning a prize to spend a month in Japan where I visited the Comme de Garcon design studio, and met the paper makers for Issey Miyake's extra-ordinary coats.

When I graduated, the lovely Anne Tyrrell was on the assessment panel. She found me my first job as Assistant Designer at the London-based Designer, Sara Sturgeon, where I spent four and a half invaluable years learning the mechanics of how the industry functioned, as I was exposed to all areas of the fashion world, from design to delivery.

This was also a period of huge personal challenge, as I grappled with who I was and whether my faith had any part to play.

image: Pedro Gabriel

when did God first appear on the stage of your life?

MANY PEOPLE DIDN'T UNDERSTAND ... HOW DID SUCH AN APPARENTLY INDULGENT WORLD LINE UP WITH MY FAITH?

The man who had received the five talents went at once and put his money to work ... His master said "well done, good and faithful servant!"

Matthew 25:16, 21

MY mother became a Christian when I was five years old. She re-married when I was nine, and my step-dad became a Christian, so faith was influential throughout my early life. I was part of a charismatic church and my active faith led me to be baptised, aged thirteen.

Many people outside of my family didn't understand why I was so passionate about fashion ... how did such an apparently indulgent world line up with my faith?

When I started seriously to consider my career, though, I sensed quite clearly God saying to me that He had given me this gift, and I should use it - Jesus' parable of the talents (*Matthew 25:14 & Luke 19:12*)

Risk your life and get more than you ever dreamed of. Luke 19:26, The Message

faith and identity at university?

IT WAS DIFFICULT TO FIND A CHURCH THAT RESPECTED THE COMMITMENTS I HAD TO MY COURSE AND STUDIES

MY faith floundered at university. It was difficult to find a church that respected the commitments I had to my course and studies. I felt disconnected. And this was just the stage in my life where I needed support, as I grappled with my identity.

I had always had a sense of being a bit different and found myself struggling with homosexual feelings, becoming emotionally detached. I had no-one to talk to about all this, and buried myself in harder and harder work - performing well in fashion was an antidote.

grappling with sexuality

AS I look back, I can see that the absence of a father figure in the early years of my life played a big part in the struggles I had with my sexuality. Yet the foundations to my faith, which they helped lay, proved to be the bedrock on which I knew, deep down, that God was my Father, who would help me through whatever was going on in my life. He was my security, as the waves of doubt and confusion swept over me - the anchor for my soul.

All of us have different battles - alcohol, drugs, food, work, sexuality ... I don't believe that God distinguishes between them. He longs for us to find our security and wholeness in Him. It won't necessarily happen overnight - it took me years to work my way through - but He is patient and will hold us as we turn, day by day, to Him.

The very facets of my character that found me having to confront my sexuality are those which define who I am - sensitive, not just being able to see beauty, but to create it with understanding and insight; prophetic words, the ability to stand alongside others.

I thank God that He has led me to understand myself better and I have been blessed with a wonderful wife and children. But I have a strong heart for those who are unclear about their sexuality, their identity, how God sees them, and whether or not He loves them.

I carried a burden of guilt and shame for many years, and my prayer is that the church will stand with those finding themselves in that place, not condemn or reject them.

we have this hope as an anchor for the soul, firm and secure.
Hebrews 6:19

THE FATHER'S SONG
THE FATHER'S LOVE
YOU SUNG IT OVER ME
AND FOR ETERNITY
IT'S WRITTEN ON
MY HEART
© *2000 Matt Redman*

ALL OF US HAVE
DIFFERENT BATTLES
- ALCOHOL, DRUGS, FOOD,
WORK, SEXUALITY ...
I DON'T BELIEVE THAT
GOD DISTINGUISHES
BETWEEN THEM

God did not send His Son into the world to condemn the world but to save the world through Him. John 3:17

SORTING OUT MY PERSONAL LIFE

WHEN I was twenty-four, I went on an Alpha course, an opportunity to explore the Christian faith with others. Through all the years of struggle, I hadn't doubted that God was there, but I hadn't allowed Him to be at the heart of my life.

When I took the step to do the course, things changed: relationships started to open up, I reconnected with friends I had grown up with at church in Plymouth, Sara Sturgeon's business moved offices and I found myself in Bermondsey, at the City Hope Church where, within just a couple of weeks, I met my wife to be.

Clare had a background in charity work, helping children with behavioural difficulties. She'd worked in Hong Kong with the renowned Jackie Pullinger, and had a real heart for the poor and marginalised. I'd never met anyone like her!

We started going out, but it would be seven years before we married; it took us that long to get to grips with the polar opposite worlds we seemed to inhabit, and I was still unravelling just who I was and trying to fathom out what the future held.

In the meantime, I moved on from Sara Sturgeon to work in Italy for two years, at MaxMara, a large, high end brand where my esrtwhile tutor at Kingston, Ian Griffiths, had been appointed Creative Director. This was an altogether bigger machine, and I was focussed purely on design. While I missed being able to turn my hand to a wide range of roles, the scene was being set for me to start my own business.

> THROUGH ALL THE YEARS OF STRUGGLE, I HADN'T DOUBTED THAT GOD WAS THERE, BUT I HADN'T ALLOWED HIM TO BE AT THE HEART OF MY LIFE

image: Pedro Gabriel

MY OWN BUSINESS

I had always wanted to start my own label, but sort of assumed that God wouldn't want that. Was it a case of thinking that God didn't want me to self promote? Whatever, there was a real drive within me and, with experience under my belt, when an opportunity came, I grasped it.

As I started to pursue this dream, I came to see that the relationships I'd been building along the way were the building blocks for my own brand. I needed to be able to manufacture, sell and make an income. The factory I'd worked with at Sara Sturgeon said they'd make the collection and, at my first meeting with them, they offered studio space in their premises, initially free of charge, and then at a nominal rent. I was there for eleven years! Finance, always a struggle for a small business, came from friends, family and my own personal savings, along with a start up bank loan. My step-brother helped me to write a business plan and with this capital it saw me through the first five years.

Initially, I showed my work privately, but then stepped up to exhibit for eight seasons at London Fashion Week. At a time when many were producing offshore, I made all my ranges in London, for the relationship with my production process was an important part of the business. Similarly the highlights of a season were receiving buyers into the showroom and seeing how they enjoyed working with the product.

The business has now evolved and I engage directly with clients at twice yearly pop up events. I am looking to have a collaborative workshop and a more permanent retail/workshop space with customers who want something unique.

image: Pedro Gabriel

image: Shaun James Cox

Daniel lecturing on creative pattern cutting at the British Fashion Council

the joys and frustrations of designing a new collection?

I love the energy of creating a garment - from the first seeds of an idea, through development and production, to someone wearing it - it's thrilling.

Working in partnership with pattern cutters and other technicians is a great experience. I so enjoy engaging with their different talents, watching my designs take shape as a 3-dimensional dress or jacket.

Yet, fashion can also be a ruthless treadmill, with this same process a trap that can drain the life out of you.

There is an addiction to the next new thing - "that's so last season!" This steals the opportunity to develop great ideas and carry them forward, crushing creativity and any longevity.

I HAD THE GIFT TO MAINTAIN RELATIONSHIPS WITH COLLEAGUES I'D WORKED WITH

I ALWAYS STOOD BY WHAT I SAID I'D DO. NOT EVERYONE HAS THIS INTEGRITY

THE BALANCE I NOW HAVE FEELS LIKE FREEDOM RATHER THAN SLAVERY

are faith, fashion & marriage compatible?

MY faith has given me the confidence - trusting that God knows best and can deliver - to step off the ladder and then step back on again. It may have restricted the growth of my business, but the balance I now have feels like freedom rather than slavery.

a final word?

IT would have been great to have a huge press profile, but I'm more about people, so this probably would not have been the best route for me. I have a real sense of God overseeing my journey and I want to align with who He's made me.

a Bible verse that has empowered your journey?

I URGE YOU ... IN VIEW OF GOD'S MERCY, TO OFFER YOUR BODIES AS LIVING SACRIFICES, HOLY AND PLEASING TO GOD ... DO NOT CONFORM TO THE PATTERN OF THIS WORLD, BUT BE TRANSFORMED BY THE RENEWING OF YOUR MIND. THEN YOU WILL BE ABLE TO TEST AND APPROVE WHAT GOD'S WILL IS - HIS GOOD, PLEASING AND PERFECT WILL

Romans 12: 1,2

image: Pedro Gabriel

AS I LOOK BACK, IT IS CLEAR THAT
GOD HAS MIRACULOUSLY SUSTAINED
MY BUSINESS. THE JOURNEY HAS HAD
MANY TWISTS AND TURNS ALONG THE
WAY AND THE PATH THAT I AM NOW
ON LOOKS QUITE DIFFERENT TO THE
PLACE FROM WHICH I SET OUT

daniel blake

A PRAYER FOR
FASHION DESIGNERS

FATHER GOD, thank you for fashion designers, who bring alive in our day, the creativity you have vested in humanity, reflecting Your own creative genius, which made us and the world in which we live.

Reveal to designers their own specific giftedness that they might walk in the path you have planned for them, not strive after a goal they are unsuited to.

Provide the resources, contacts and wisdom those already working need to grow and develop, steering them to use their gifts in a way that honours the Giver and creates clothes that bring pleasure and identity to those that wear them.

Give courage and determination to those setting out on their careers, that they might pursue their dream and not be deterred by the challenges they face, or those around them who might not understand their vision and passion.
Amen

FIONA DIEFFENBACHER

image: Zhi Wei

Fiona is the programme director for BFA Fashion Design in the School of Fashion, Parsons School of Design. The programme's rich legacy boasts an impressive roster of alumni who have defined the US fashion industry from Claire McCardell and Donna Karan to Marc Jacobs and Alexander Wang. In her role, Fiona oversees every aspect of programme delivery including the implementation of new curriculum, faculty, student life, governance, and all related events.

WHILE THE DESIGN PROCESS IS
FUNDAMENTAL TO THE WAY ALL
FASHION DESIGNERS WORK, THERE
IS NO RIGHT OR WRONG METHOD

STARTING OUT ...

fiona's story

I grew up in Belfast, Northern Ireland, in the midst of what are often referred to as 'the Troubles' – an environment hardly conducive to fostering a dream of fashion. Yet, my path was apparent from an early age. At seven, I was figuring out how to make clothes for my dolls; cutting and sewing my own patterns by age eleven - and all the time, dreaming of becoming a fashion designer.

This began to become a reality when I was selected, as one of only eight, into the BA Honours degree in Textiles and Fashion at the University of Ulster. During my time in the programme, I was chosen to represent Northern Ireland as a UK Smirnoff Award semi-finalist, and my graduate collection was showcased at the Gilbey's Fashion Awards in Dublin.

After graduation, I headed to London with a couple of classmates and, nine months later, made the impromptu decision to join a friend, who had secured a summer internship in New York. He hated the city, quit his internship and left after two weeks. I, on the other hand, never looked back. I was intrigued by all New York had to offer. I kept hearing about Parsons School of Design, and decided to set up an appointment with an advisor, to discuss the possibilities of taking a class or two to help me gain an entry point into the industry.

MY MOTHER
OFTEN QUOTED
THE SAYING:
*THURSDAY'S CHILD
HAS FAR TO GO ...*
AND THIS HAS BEEN
TRUE OF MY LIFE
JOURNEY THUS FAR

What followed was an unprecedented chain of events: I met with the Chair of the BFA Fashion Department, who offered me a place in the programme on the spot. I told him I didn't want to undertake another degree and couldn't afford the fees as an international student, so he quickly called financial aid, who confirmed the offer of a merit scholarship. They called him back, before the end of my interview, to offer me more money (something unheard of). He looked up and asked me: "Do you go to church? Because this NEVER happens!" I told him I was a Christian and, at that point, I knew beyond a shadow of doubt that God was at work directing me in this next phase of my journey.

45

MY OWN LABEL ... FIONA WALKER

CLIENTS NOTED
THAT THERE WAS
"SOMETHING
DIFFERENT"
ABOUT ME AS
A DESIGNER
- NO EGO,
NO PRETENSION,
DOWN TO EARTH,
AND NOT CAUGHT
UP IN THE CIRCUS
THAT IS FASHION

*image: Fall 1999 South of Seventh Show
Randy Brooke*

I thrived at Parsons and, as a graduating senior in 1993, I won Michael Kors' Designer of the Year Award and went on to work as a knitwear designer in the industry for five years, before starting my own label (Fiona Walker). In 1998. God gave me a vision to create a new business model - one that was built on biblical principles, with integrity at every level - from the choice of fabrics, sample rooms and production facilities, to how I treated my team (clients, interns, models, PR, sales).

It was an incredible journey and, even without speaking overtly about my faith, people noted the difference in my approach. I treated the models at my casting call as people not objects, looking at their books and offering feedback; even if I wasn't selecting them for the show. My store became a sanctuary where women felt at ease to share deep concerns that went beyond mere retail therapy. Clients noted that there was 'something different' about me as a designer - no ego, no pretension, down to earth, and not caught up in the circus that is fashion. We opened a small showroom/studio in Hell's Kitchen (!) and showed at New York Fashion Week, garnering press from The New York Times, Harpers Bazaar, WWD and other key publications.

During this time, I maintained my connection to Parsons - acting as an External Critic to the third year students, and selecting the best talent from the class as the recipient of the Fiona Walker 'Silver Thimble Award'. I was encouraged by the team at Parsons to think about teaching - but wasn't able to commit as the business was gathering momentum and we had begun building our wholesale business, distributing the collection via retail avenues in the U.S. and Japan. As the business grew, the financial pressures were constant, the competition was fierce and the struggle to balance the industry's idols of ego and recognition remained daily challenges for me.

It was September 2001.

setting up your own label couldn't have been easy ...

FOR many fashion designers, the ultimate success is to have your own label and I was no different. As a Christian, I knew the pressure of proving myself every season, to an industry that would discard me the moment the next new designer came along, was all too real and that I needed to stay focused on what really mattered - God's purpose for my life.

The cash flow was incredibly challenging, and I quickly learned that C.O.D (Cash on Demand) didn't really exist, as shady vendors post-dated bad cheques, which meant I was quickly operating at a deficit, while they sold my product and profited. My commitment to running a business with integrity was challenged every day. How did I honour that promise? It meant that practically, I honoured my payments, even when others were failing to do so to me.

And then, being a woman in business was very difficult, and it's sad to say that gender inequality is alive and well. I had to learn how to negotiate, to push for what I wanted and to stand my ground. But, when it came to delinquent invoices, no matter how tough I was, the fact remained that vendors responded to a man more than a woman, and I often had to involve my husband to resolve late payment issues.

As a newcomer and potential emerging talent, many sought to join in my early success, some legitimate - others not. I remember, in my eagerness to grow the business, I entered into an agreement with a showroom - ignoring my gut instinct and all the red flags. It was a disaster! I watched as an incompetent sales-person destroyed a key vendor relationship in a matter of minutes - never to be redeemed.

THERE WERE MANY DARK MOMENTS WHERE WE HIT ROCK BOTTOM FINANCIALLY ... YET GOD CONTINUED TO PROVIDE

do not worry, saying: "what shall we eat", "what shall we drink", "what shall we wear". Seek first His kingdom and His righteousness and all these things will be given to you as well. Matthew 6:33

did you sense God at work through these dark times?

LOOKING back on the seven years in business, I know God used my brokenness to show me His glory; I saw Him use the trials we faced, to teach me how to depend on Him alone as my security, rather than the unpredictability of my bank balance. There were many dark moments, where we hit rock bottom financially ... yet God continued to provide. These remain in our memory as markers of His faithfulness.

At the bleakest of these times, we turned to Him in prayer and to our community who prayed with and for us. They truly demonstrated the body of Christ, carrying our burdens when we needed them most.

47

THEN 9/11 HAPPENED ...

ALONG with the devastation that changed our lives and New York forever that day, in the aftermath, I (along with so many others) was faced with a business that came to a crashing halt, as one vendor after another contacted me saying they couldn't pay our invoice, or that they were closing/declaring bankruptcy etc.

What was I going to do? We had to think on our feet to stay afloat. We negotiated a greatly reduced rent with our landlord, switched our business model from wholesale to retail, created a vintage line called 'Retro Redux' and spent our time shopping for vintage finds, out-of-state, that we could mark up and sell in the boutique. We diversified our product offerings and sold local designer goods (accessories, jewellery and gift-wear). We deconstructed, dyed and reconstructed items, customized t-shirts and offered knitting classes and workshops in the back of the store. Our business model was re-imagined.

In 2002, our lease was up and we moved to a new retail space further uptown, and I saw this as a new beginning. We put all our efforts (and dwindling funds) into the re-modelling of the space, and production of the collection.

Over the next three years, the store was a success - this new location drew a clientele that were more aligned with our brand identity. We had loyal followers who supported us 1000%, but we quickly encountered a new problem - inventory re-stocking. When we sold out of items, I couldn't develop new prototypes fast enough to meet the consumer demand for newness. If a customer bought an item and came back two weeks later, I had to have something new in the store to generate return business. But it wasn't feasible, because our cash flow was so tight, and it became apparent that this was not a viable model.

WE HAD TO
THINK ON OUR
FEET TO STAY
AFLOAT

OUR CASH FLOW
WAS SO TIGHT ...
IT BECAME
APPARENT THAT
THIS WAS NOT
A VIABLE MODEL

did you find yourself grappling with God in these testing days?

WHEN we set up a new store, I remember a good friend (and pastor) prayed for God's will to be done, even if the store wasn't a success. I remember my heart jolting, as I struggled to agree. In that moment, my true heart's desire was revealed - I was still seeking success more than God.

Eventually, our financial debt, leftover from 9/11, proved insurmountable. No matter how hard we tried, we could no longer sustain the momentum needed to generate new product and keep the business afloat. I knew the writing was on the wall, but I was still clinging desperately to the dream.

Late one night, in February 2005, I heard that unmistakeable, still, small voice saying to me: "You want this more than me, and it must go."

This realisation hit me at my very core, and I wept bitterly. When I went into the store the next day and faced the reality of all I was giving up, I locked the door, turned off the lights, and sat in the dark, mourning the death of my dream.

Eventually, I came to terms with what God was doing in my heart. He was dethroning the self-filled dream of success and the glory I wanted for myself, and replacing it with Himself. He had so very graciously given me my dream in all its fullness for seven years and, in the process, he had worked to refine my heart, in readiness for the next phase of the journey.

image: Anja Ligtenberg

Jesus often withdrew to lonely places and prayed Luke 5:16

FIONA has been described as a hybrid personality made up of equal parts extrovert and introvert. While loving the vibrant experiences NYC has to offer she also enjoys quiet solitude to recharge and bring a sense of equilibrium to life.

I HEARD THAT
STILL, SMALL VOICE:
"YOU WANT THIS
MORE THAN ME
AND IT MUST GO"
... I WEPT BITTERLY

49

INTO EDUCATION ...

AFTER we closed the business in 2005, I began freelancing and recalled the earlier proposal to teach. So, I walked across the street to Parsons, hoping to speak with Tim Gunn (the then Chair of the BFA Fashion Design program). He wasn't available, because he was filming the first season of Project Runway. But, as I turned to leave, he walked right out of the elevator, and we had an impromptu meeting, where he offered me a teaching position. That was June, and two months later I began teaching two design concepts classes. Six years later, I became the Programme Director – essentially the same job Tim had.

My journey had come full circle back to Parsons. Even though I never thought of teaching, God gave me a fresh vision for fashion in the context of education, to use all that I had learned as an entrepreneur to impact the next generation of talent within the industry.

In 2013, my first publication - Fashion Thinking: Creative Approaches to the Design Process - sought to unmask varied approaches to design, enabling designers to better understand their own ways of working.

My recent research project , 'Dress and Emotion", launched in February 2015, investigates clothing as a means of identity and communication.

Ultimately, I view my vocation as a calling and, throughout my life, I have tried to follow God's leading, because I know his purposes are ultimately greater than my own. My vision for cultural renewal in the area of Fashion Design has evolved over the past decade as an educator, but God's call for me to work in fashion was present from the very beginning.

Never underestimate the power of God to place you where He wants in order to establish his purposes for His glory.

NEVER UNDERESTIMATE THE POWER OF GOD TO PLACE YOU WHERE HE WANTS

3 great things about working in fashion education?

THE STUDENTS: helping them discover who they are, harnessing their strengths, witnessing their evolution, revelations, successes, and transition into professional life.

THE CULTURE: being engaged in education keeps you sharply focused on the space in between industry and academia - it forces you to push the boundaries, in order to cultivate new methods at the intersections of pedagogy, research and industry practice, within the fashion context.

THE FUTURE: education has the ability to imagine the future, to embrace new technologies and prototype possibilities within the classroom 'lab' setting. It seeks to address existing problems and generate solutions and new modes of thinking, that will ultimately redefine the industry.

EDUCATION HAS THE ABILITY TO IMAGINE THE FUTURE, TO EMBRACE NEW TECHNOLOGIES, AND PROTOTYPE POSSIBILITIES WITHIN THE CLASSROOM 'LAB' SETTING

God's top commandment for fashion?

THOU SHALT NOT STEAL

The fashion industry needs to respect intellectual property and support original design, respect the human rights of the workers to earn a fair wage and be treated with dignity.

3 things you'd like to change in fashion education?

PERCEPTION: Fashion is often perceived as a non-academic discipline and, as a result, our significant contributions to the field often go unrecognised, in terms of the depth and breadth of practice, across not only design, but within applied research contexts.

COMMUNITY: Fashion, as an industry, has a reputation of being competitive and cut-throat. As educators, we have the opportunity to train students to create and celebrate community, moving away from the 'I' towards the 'we'. At Parsons, we have already begun to achieve this, as students form strong familial bonds and seek one another's success, as much as their own.

COLLABORATION: Fashion often stands apart from other disciplines, and is perceived as inward facing. This is something that needs to change in the academic context, as we seek to build a more collaborative model moving forward, where cross-pollination occurs toward building hybrid practices and peer to peer proposals.

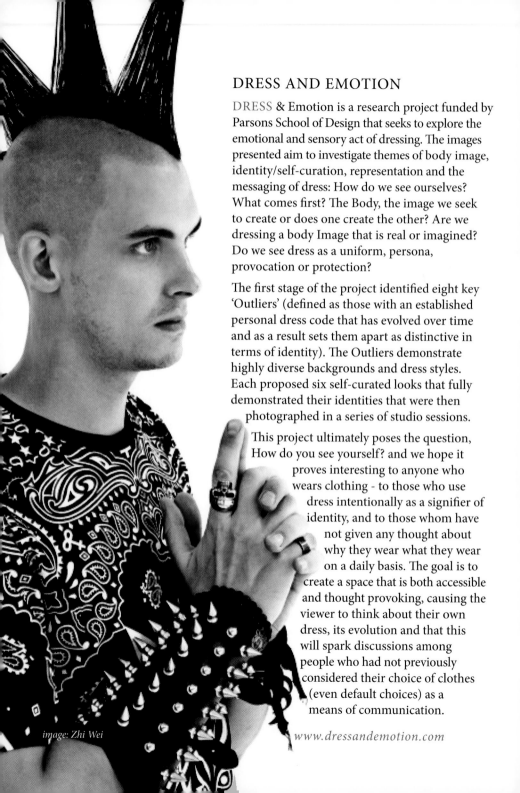

DRESS AND EMOTION

DRESS & Emotion is a research project funded by Parsons School of Design that seeks to explore the emotional and sensory act of dressing. The images presented aim to investigate themes of body image, identity/self-curation, representation and the messaging of dress: How do we see ourselves? What comes first? The Body, the image we seek to create or does one create the other? Are we dressing a body Image that is real or imagined? Do we see dress as a uniform, persona, provocation or protection?

The first stage of the project identified eight key 'Outliers' (defined as those with an established personal dress code that has evolved over time and as a result sets them apart as distinctive in terms of identity). The Outliers demonstrate highly diverse backgrounds and dress styles. Each proposed six self-curated looks that fully demonstrated their identities that were then photographed in a series of studio sessions.

This project ultimately poses the question, How do you see yourself? and we hope it proves interesting to anyone who wears clothing - to those who use dress intentionally as a signifier of identity, and to those whom have not given any thought about why they wear what they wear on a daily basis. The goal is to create a space that is both accessible and thought provoking, causing the viewer to think about their own dress, its evolution and that this will spark discussions among people who had not previously considered their choice of clothes (even default choices) as a means of communication.

image: Zhi Wei

www.dressandemotion.com

FASHION THINKING:

CREATIVE APPROACHES
TO THE DESIGN PROCESS

DESIGNERS are problem-solvers. On the macro level tackling issues of sustainability, safety, disability, beauty, diversity and body image as the focus of their work. Then begins the challenge of problem solving on the micro level; in the incremental decisions of research, ideation, fabric innovation, prototyping, fit and so on.

Design is ultimately about choices; these run subconsciously through the mind of a designer, as they move through each stage in the design process.

Initially for students, while they are trying to figure out their aesthetic and articulate their voice, it is equally important for them to discover their working methodology.

Someone asked me why I called the book 'Fashion Thinking?' I replied "Because students don't!" Not because they lack intelligence or capacity - but because they don't stop to reflect on their work at each stage in order to think critically about the concept, the ideation, what's working, what's not and, in the final analysis, they don't know why something is good. The ability to identify, analyse, and reflect is central to students' ability to self-assess and edit their own work on an ongoing basis.

WE are all familiar with the phrase 'think outside the box'. But what if there is no box? What if the box (whether you are inside or outside) is the problem itself?

The impetus for my book grew out of my teaching practice, where students struggle not only to discover their strengths and develop a unique design aesthetic, but also to understand their own process and working methodology.

Texts addressing fashion design at that time missed the mark, as they took a narrow approach that appeared formulaic; ('draw it, make it', mood-board, fabrics, flats, etc) they tended to showcase projects in their final stage of completion, without unmasking the real process of design, or the varied ways to enter into that process. This approach trains students in a rote manner, that pre-determines outcomes and sends them ill-prepared into an already staid industry, that needs to re-think it's approach to design in terms of upending traditional techniques and move towards generating newness and innovation.

As educators, it is incumbent upon us to stay ahead of the curve, and embrace new innovations in our field that are occurring at an ever-increasing rate. Our students arrive with radically different skill-sets than five years ago (even a year ago). The Millennials live in a fully synthesized digital world, with very few reference points to analog modes of working. Therefore, our approach to curriculum, and how we teach design in this context needs to adapt quickly.

image: James Ewing

THE ABILITY TO IDENTIFY, ANALYSE,
AND REFLECT IS CENTRAL TO
STUDENTS' ABILITY TO SELF-ASSESS
AND EDIT THEIR OWN WORK

fiona dieffenbacher

A PRAYER FOR
FASHION EDUCATORS

LORD, remind me that I am here to serve with
excellence. May I be an example to my students as
I seek to lead with integrity, honour and humility.

Give me your vision for each student - insight into
every individual need, intuition to know when to
push and when to hold back, and understanding
on how to guide each one forward.

Help me to remember that each student is created
in your image and that my role is merely to bring
out the gifts you have already bestowed.

Provide me with patience for those who are slow
to learn, capacity to spur the most talented on to
greater heights, and the ability to speak the truth
in love at all times.

Keep me from showing favouritism; may I seek to
balance grace and mercy with justice and parity,
as I assess student work and progress.

Give me your joy as I approach each class, and if
I grow weary, give me your strength to continue
to lead my students with confidence.

I ask that you build character as well as skills,
strengthen hearts as well as minds, as they move
through their academic journey.

By the grace of the Lord Jesus Christ. Amen

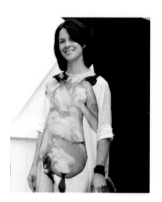

AMANDA KING

Amanda has worked as a designer for the high street, created her own collections and worked in sales for leading British designers. She has a passion to pray without ceasing for all those, including Christians, who work in fashion.

I LOVED THE COLOUR & TEXTURE
BEING MESSY, PAINTING,
CREATING COLLAGES

AN EARLY PASSION FOR ART ...

amanda's story

I wanted to be a fine artist at school. They suggested I become a teacher, but it was not something that I was excited about at the time. I did History of Art and Art at A level, and loved the colour and texture, being messy, painting, creating collages.

I was going to do an Art Foundation course in Bournemouth but, due to a last minute change of plan, ended up in Hounslow.

Even though it was not a well-known college, it was brilliant - so much time to experiment, creating sculpture, print making, photography, huge pictures with ripped card painted all over. "Heh, you'd be good at Textiles", said my tutor, which had evolved to: "Why not go into fashion?" by the end of the course.

St Martins seemed very daunting when I visited, and I ended up in the green fields of Kent, at Ravensbourne. I turned up for interview with a huge portfolio of art, including some of the worst fashion sketches you'll ever see. But they liked it, and I had a great time there, studying Printed Textiles and Fashion Design.

In my final year, I won a competition, supported by Lycra and The Observer, for a lightweight travel wardrobe. The judges included Bodymap and Lucille Lewin from Whistles. The prize was to have part of the collection sold in Whistles. When they asked for my patterns, I was too scared to give them. I didn't think pattern cutting was my forte. In retrospect, I realised this was a missed opportunity.

as a teenager was it easy pursuing a creative career?

IT was not at problem at home, and I was fully encouraged. I had been a Christian since I was thirteen, and belonged to a church that had a strong missionary focus, with doctors and teachers going to far-flung places to care for people and spread the good news of Jesus Christ. So, I wondered if the creative path was the right one for me, as I too had a missionary heart. It took me a while to realise that I could do the same in the fashion industry, using the creative gifts I had been given.

> I WONDERED IF THE CREATIVE PATH WAS THE RIGHT ONE FOR ME, AS I TOO HAD A MISSIONARY HEART

any advice to young people setting out?

GO FOR WHAT YOU ARE PASSIONATE ABOUT. NOT WHAT OTHER PEOPLE SAY YOU SHOULD BE DOING - HOWEVER WELL-MEANING THEY MIGHT BE. DON'T GET DISCOURAGED, KEEP TRYING, PUSHING DOORS, PRAYING AS YOU GO. GOD HAS THE BEST PLAN FOR YOU

your faith has always been central

MY faith is key each day. I never really know where or when my next job will come from, and trust that God does. Amazing things have happened when I have prayed, let go of worry, and placed it in God's hands. I have then seen doors open, some of which I've never even pushed.

I often found myself reminded of Jesus' Parable of the Talents, and how those who put what they were given to best use were commended. It's not what you've got, but what you do with it that counts. I always felt strongly about using my talents well, and asking "What should I be doing?"

> "MASTER, YOU ENTRUSTED ME WITH FIVE TALENTS. SEE I HAVE GAINED FIVE MORE." THE MASTER REPLIED: "WELL DONE GOOD AND FAITHFUL SERVANT. I WILL PUT YOU IN CHARGE OF MANY THINGS."
>
> *Matthew 25:20,21*

CHALLENGES IN THE WORKPLACE ...

AFTER graduation, I did a variety of jobs: designing two collections for a high street retailer; creating illustrations for BT; lecturing in Art & Design at Kingston FE College.

1994 saw me getting married to Jon, and I thought it was time I 'got a proper job'. I secured a position for a UK company, as the sole designer with a team of buyers, travelling around factories in Leicester and London. The working conditions I encountered shocked me and, with an increasing amount of production going offshore, there was real sense of depression around. I could not believe how we treated people in this country.

As I went to Spring Harvest that year, I had a clear sense that I wanted to get out of this industry. The poor conditions I had seen left me with a real sense that I wanted to run from the problem. The injustice in the industry seemed hopeless. Did I want to belong to an industry that treated people this way? I wondered just what it was I had been involved in. God, though, had different ideas!

I had a vivid encounter with God - *see next page: how does God speak to you?* - and I just knew that He wanted me to stay where I was, in Fashion. A verse quoted in one of the talks at Spring Harvest got under my skin - *God said to Moses: "Go, set my people free".* This was to be the springboard for what came next.

The context of the verse was the Israelites enduring centuries of slavery in ancient Egypt under the despotic Pharaoh. While praying after the talk, I had a picture of women in India in a factory. This reminded me of a project a friend had told me about before, and I knew I had to contact them.

I soon found myself in touch with a lady, Ruth Cox, who had started the Oasis project in Mumbai called Jacobs Well.

I THOUGHT
IT WAS TIME I
GOT A PROPER JOB

I HAD A CLEAR SENSE
THAT I WANTED TO GET
OUT OF THIS INDUSTRY.
GOD, THOUGH, HAD
DIFFERENT IDEAS!

Go, I am sending you to Pharaoh to bring my people the Israelites out of Egypt ... I will be with you.
Exodus 3:10:12

how does God speak to you?

IN 1994, there was a real move of the Holy Spirit in the UK, and I longed to get closer to God. At Spring Harvest that year, I was all at sea about working in fashion. One evening, I left a meeting early, and returned to my chalet, completely confused.

I lay on my bed and was crying out to God to meet with me and give me strength to continue. I felt my body being filled with strength; it was strange, but amazing. As I sat up, I felt as if something red was touching my lips. A sudden thought occurred: 'that's in the Bible; where is it, Lord?' As I picked up the Bible beside me, I searched in Jeremiah thinking that happened to him and then, when I could not find it there, I said, "stuff it Lord, I can't find it". When I opened my eyes again my thumb was pointing at it in Isaiah 6: '... *one of the seraphs flew to me with a live coal in his hand ... With it he touched my lips ... I heard the voice of the Lord saying, "Whom shall I send?" ... I said "Here I am, send me."* ' (v.6-8)

I knew God wanted me where I was, that He had a specific plan for me, and that it might just include speaking to people!

I KNEW GOD WANTED ME WHERE I WAS, THAT HE HAD A SPECIFIC PLAN FOR ME, AND THAT IT MIGHT JUST INCLUDE SPEAKING TO PEOPLE!

early engagement with Christians in fashion?

AT Art College, I had put a note up on the board: 'Calling all Christians!' Then, at Greenbelt Festival, I helped for a number of years organising the fashion show and ran a stall selling different designers' designs. As I came across more and more Christians in fashion who were struggling and needed support, I realised I needed to be doing something more strategic. I asked God what this might look like and suddenly people started appearing.

We met at a friend's flat to chat and pray. It turned out that this was the beginning of an ongoing calling to stand alongside those working in fashion.

TO INDIA & BOURNEMOUTH ...

JACOBS WELL is an NGO-led exploration into meaningful employment opportunities for women living in slums, and those vulnerable to different forms of discrimination, abuse, violence and exploitation. Initially, I served on their Advisory Committee in the UK but, when they asked me to design a collection and work for them, I was thrilled. This felt like it was bringing together my heart for justice and for fashion.

I went out to India for two weeks. I was very kindly lent a beige Salwar Kameez suit. I remember thinking: 'beige is definitely not my colour!' The first day, I met the women from Jacobs Well on the train on the way to work. They were adorned in vibrant, beautiful colours - and had faces full of joy. I was struck by the contrast between my rather complaining attitude and the radiance of these women, who were still living in slums. I resolved never to moan again!

When I returned to the UK, I spoke, with all the passion I could muster, to churches and all who would listen, about how God was at work in fashion.

Some time later, as I watched a video of a Jacobs Well show in Mumbai for wealthy clients, my heart jumped. At the end of the show, all the women who had made the clothes walked up the catwalk and took the traditional bow. How delighted they looked at the applause they received. How thrilled I was that they received the honour for all their hard work. What a wonderful model - but how rarely is it followed.

He raises the poor from the dust and lifts the needy from the ash heap;
He seats them with princes, with the princes of their people. Psalm 113:7-8
Or (from THE MESSAGE version) *He picks up the poor from out of the dirt,*
rescues the wretched who've been thrown out with the trash. Seats them among
the honoured guests, a place of honour among the brightest and the best.

Back at home, Jon and I discussed moving from London, down to Bournemouth. I had picked up an illness whilst travelling around France in our camper van (normally caught in Africa!) I needed to recuperate and Jasmine was only six months old at the time. Jon took a job in Southampton and we joined a church that met in a pub. It was called BLISS! Soon after we became part of BLISS, we listened to a talk based on a passage in the book of Haggai, entitled 'Build my church'.

God was on my case again.

Jacobs Well and fair trade

THE Jacobs Well journey started in Mumbai in 1994. From humble beginnings as a tailoring unit engaging in embroidery, pattern making, cutting and machining, the project quickly grew, creating an in-house brand of products and setting up a further training and production unit in Bangalore. As the company continues to grow, new training and production initiatives are being explored with the hope of setting up partner organisations with the same high standards in further communities across India and Nepal.

With sustainable principles at the heart of its endeavours, membership of the World Fair Trade Organisation in 2009 gave Jacobs Well the recognised credibility to highlight its good practice, confirming that it:

- never employs or outsources to child labour
- always pay fair wages
- has safe and good working conditions for all workers

Jacobs Well is registered with the Ethical Fashion Forum and has added its voice to the annual Fashion Revolution Day. As pioneers in the ethical fashion movement, the company plays an active part celebrating a fashion industry that prizes fairness at all stages of the production chain.

CELEBRATING A FASHION INDUSTRY THAT PRIZES FAIRNESS AT ALL STAGES OF THE PRODUCTION CHAIN

I made your clothes!
#FASHREV

FASHION REVOLUTION

WHO MADE MY CLOTHES?
24.04.15
#FASHREV

... BACK TO LONDON ...

I threw myself into the church in Bournemouth, helping extend its facilities above the pub, and my studio ended up being there. They were good days; establishing a family and growing in faith. We were there for five years.

One day, I had a mental picture of the women in the Cabinet War Rooms pushing ships and troops around a table map. I strongly felt that I needed to be on the spot, where the action was taking place. I reckoned that London Fashion Week was a key focus for the fashion industry, and gathered a few friends together to pray around the edges of the event for all those taking part. It was time to return to London.

I thought about writing to the organisers, the British Fashion Council, to ask if I could come inside to pray for everyone. Who should I meet shortly afterwards? The BFC's Chief Operating Officer, Simon Ward (author of this book!). A guest pass was arranged, and I was in!

Speaking to people at London Fashion Week, I found myself meeting some great designers and people working in the industry, and one lady in particular, Philippa Prior, who helped to host guests of the principal sponsor of LFW. She later offered me the job, and it was mine for seven years. It was an amazing role, meeting some lovely guests who I took to the catwalk shows and told them about the industry. I got to meet many of the designers, was chatting to people all day long, and had access to lovely food. It was perfect!

I always worried, though, that this opportunity was only two weeks a year. What about the rest of the time? God was on the case. I had met Anne Tyrrell, a wonderful connector and former BFC Vice Chairman. She suggested my growing knowledge and communication skills were perfect to help designers with their sales.

I NEEDED TO BE ON THE SPOT, WHERE THE ACTION WAS TAKING PLACE

A prophetic friend prayed over me and had a picture of me ice skating on frozen canals in Amsterdam ... I was saying "hi", "hi", "hi" to everyone I came across.

I felt this job was like that prophectic picture, the start of meeting lots of people in the industry and getting a heart for those who work in it.

One link that thrilled me was with the security guards at London Fashion Week. I spent much time hanging around chatting to them (between shows, of course), and it was a real privilege to share their problems and pray with some of them - on one occasion resulting in the miraculous healing of a guard's foot. God is good.

Artisan Fashion Group

STEVE COLE is a great connector who, in 1997, had set up Artisan, a networking group to support Christians across the media, arts and fashion industries. It's three guiding principles were:

UNITY – isolation can be good, but not all the time, we need one another.

HUMILITY – we are important, but we recognise our place and dependency.

PRAYER – the centre of operations. Prayer does not equip us for greater works ... prayer is the greater work.

I have been involved with Artisan from the start. When I returned to London, Steve and I were at the same church, St Mary's Bryanston Square, and Artisan seemed the perfect umbrella under which to bring together all the Christians I had been meeting over the years. The Artisan Fashion Group included designers, journalists, photographers ... people from all areas of the industry. It was here that someone prophesied over me that I would spread my networking and prayer cover to Paris and LA.

juggling children and work ...

IT can be a real challenge being a working mum. I have been fortunate, in that Jon and I have been able to share childcare when our children were pre-school, and now I have great support from parents at school, who help out when I need it.

I decided not to go back into full time work after our three children had all arrived. For some, I know, this would be a real sacrifice, but I have enjoyed the variety and mix of people I have been able to meet with this more flexible approach.

... AND ONWARDS TO PARIS

TALKING to many of the emerging (New Gen) designers at London Fashion Week, I got to see how important it was for their growth to sell during Paris Fashion Week (as well as showing in London). So, I decided to buy a ticket to Paris, get out there, and start praying outside the shows.

A friend, Jo Knight, who worked with Richard Nicoll, invited me to sleep on her hotel room floor. It was a short connection to helping out at Richard's showroom. Visits to the BFC's LONDON show ROOMS, where the best of London's emerging talent were based, opened doors to helping out on sales for Roksanda and Jonathan Saunders.

I have been working in Sales for the last four years, four times a year in Paris, spending as much of my spare time as I can simply speaking to designers, encouraging them and showing kindness on what is a long, eight day haul in Paris for them. It can be a stressful and sometimes slightly unreal world.

I love meeting buyers from all around the world. Theirs is not an easy role: they have tight budgets, so can't pick all they would like to, they travel so much, have frantic schedules and have a responsibility that what they choose will sell.

I believe God wants me to stand alongside these lovely people, sharing laughter and tears, showing God's lavish love and praying for them ... being an influence to the influencers.

What next? I still have on my heart Jesus' words to the apostle Peter, "Feed my sheep". Who knows where it might take me. But I hope I'm brave enough to go wherever God leads me.

I DECIDED TO BUY A TICKET TO PARIS, GET OUT THERE AND START PRAYING OUTSIDE THE SHOWS

"PARIS - A KEY TREND CAME THROUGH THE INTERNATIONAL COLLECTIONS - REAL CLOTHES. REAL CLOTHES FOR REAL WOMEN DESIGNED BY A NEW GENERATION IN TOUCH WITH REALITY"
Lewis Alexander
LA briefing Summer 2015

your favourite phrase?
GOD IS GOOD!

You're here to be light, bringing out the God-colours in the world. God is not a secret to be kept ...
Matthew 5:14 The Message

BEING AN INFLUENCE TO THE INFLUENCERS

"FEED MY SHEEP." WHO KNOWS
WHERE IT MIGHT TAKE ME. BUT
I HOPE I'M BRAVE ENOUGH TO
GO WHEREVER GOD LEADS ME

amanda king

A PRAYER FOR PEOPLE WORKING IN FASHION

FATHER GOD, You are so good!
If we would but come to You with
all that goes on in our lives, You
will guide and strengthen us for
the way ahead.

Keep drawing us back to Yourself,
that we might walk life's path hand
in hand with You.

Watch over, guide and strengthen all
those working in the many different
areas of fashion, from buyers to security
guards, designers to embroiderers,
journalists to sponsors.

May each be blessed by their encounter
with the world of fashion and protected
from the challenges it can inevitably
bring.

Shine Your light on all who work with
the interests of their colleagues in
mind, and draw to Yourself those
who cannot always see beyond what
they are doing.

All this, that fashion might increasingly
become a force for good in a broken
and needy world. Amen

SARAH McCOWEN

Sarah is a Senior Designer for a UK high street retailer. She studied Fashion Womenswear at university and went on to work with British designers before joining the high street.

THIS WAS SO LIKE GOD: STEERING ME
TOWARDS SOMETHING I HAD NEVER
CONSIDERED, BUT WHICH WAS
JUST RIGHT FOR ME

EARLY YEARS & UNIVERSITY ...

sarah's story

I remember my grandmother sewing and making us clothes when we were young. There were always fabrics around the house and all my party dresses came from her, so it was hardly surprising this influenced me as I grew up and learnt to enjoy craft, making and sewing things. My parents were also a big influence. My father had followed his heart and love of sport and worked in the sports industry. He encouraged me to do things I enjoyed.

The school I attended was more traditional and academic than vocational and, as I began to think about University, I was conscious that I had to decide whether fashion was to stay as a 'hobby', or become my career. With my parent's encouragement I decided to go for it, and applied for a fashion foundation course at Kingston University, which led to a BA in Fashion Womenswear at the University of Westminster in Harrow.

Under the guidance of an inspiring tutor, I knew I had made the right decision and, while I was there, undertook several work placements including New York, Italy, and two weeks in Hong Kong where I stayed with a Filipino lady, who was also a Christian. She said grace before meals and would play worship music to lull us to sleep each night. My faith upbringing had been traditional Church of England, with hymns and liturgy, so it was wonderful to see faith out there in everyday life and across the globe.

from CofE school to university ... was God still around?

HAVING grown up in a Church of England school with strong underlying Christian values, art college and then university life was, at first, quite a shock to the system, as I discovered that many people had little or no faith reference in their lives.

My school motto, 'may love always lead us', had stayed with me and was a good foundation for embracing all the different people around me, learning about them and seeing that our differences were not there to define us, rather to teach us and help us grow.

I truly sensed God's protection, as He sent me a close friend and confidante in a fellow student, who I am still close with, and has gone on to be a leading writer and journalist.

amor nos sempre ducat
may love always lead us
SCHOOL MOTTO

I TRULY SENSED GOD'S PROTECTION AS HE SENT ME A CLOSE FRIEND AND CONFIDANTE IN A FELLOW STUDENT

looking back, what would you say to your younger self?

let us not give up meeting together, as some are in the habit of doing, but let us encourage one another

Hebrews 10:25

AT times, I allowed myself to get wrapped up in the newness and change that came with my university life, and spent long, long hours in the studio. I didn't consider the risk to my faith, and wish I'd joined the Christian Union. It is inevitable we will be influenced by the immediate, and what is going on around us, so I didn't notice how I was missing the encouragement of those who also knew Jesus as friend and Saviour.

God was faithful to me, though, and sent another great friend, a mature student with a warm down-to-earth faith, and I was touched when she shared that her parents had been praying for their kids every day and encouraged me not to forget to ask for His guidance through prayer.

AND SO TO WORK …

ON graduation, I was fortunate and went straight into working as studio assistant with a designer, working on the embroidery on her show and production pieces for London Fashion Week.

I heard that another designer, with whom I'd done a work experience placement, was looking for an assistant. I jumped at the opportunity and, before I knew it, I had a new job. I just loved the glamour, the drama, the buzz and the energy that flowed into every aspect of the business, and how my boss took a real interest in the lives of the people working with him.

As a relatively new designer, and with me newly graduated, I took a pay cut knowing the riches of experience would outweigh short term financial gain. I embarked on an adventure, where I could be a vital part of a team, and my family were supportive, giving me the confidence to follow my heart through this opportunity.

It was an amazing learning curve but, after six years, I began to ask myself where I was going. We were a small team and I was working as studio manager, liaising with sample machinists, pattern cutters, specialist knitters, an Italian factory, sales agent, private clients, stylists, PR companies, as well as assisting with design. Every day was different, and I longed for a more structured role where there was room for personal growth.

In search of some answers, a year or two previously, I had done an Alpha course, and read John Ortberg's book, *If you want to walk on water, you have to get out of the boat*. I realised that working where I was had become my boat!

71

are long working hours inevitable in fashion?

AS a twenty-something, I loved the excitement, camaraderie and buzz of working all hours, as part of a team in the run up to show time, and truly believe this was an amazing start.

But, I did not want to find myself burnt out before I reached my full potential. Everything happens for a reason, and I wanted to find a better work-life balance, so I could contribute my whole heart to both.

Creativity doesn't have a time limit, and small businesses often have to work all hours, especially in the run up to Fashion Week. Sometimes, though, you need the structure of a big corporation to enable your imagination to take flight. I was lucky to learn who I was in this creative bubble, but I chose to get out of the boat I had been in, and find a new challenge. You have to find what fits best for you.

I LOVED THE EXCITEMENT CAMARADERIE AND BUZZ OF WORKING ALL HOURS AS PART OF A TEAM IN THE RUN UP TO SHOW TIME

should Christians work in fashion?

GOD put a desire in my heart to work with creativity and with creatives; it simply reflects our Creator.

It is a privilege to work closely alongside people contributing to the vibrancy of life, and I try to bring a caring approach where it's easy to be taken-over by the task at hand.

FASHION CHAMPIONS ALL SORTS OF CHARACTERS, FROM A WIDE VARIETY OF BACKGROUNDS, AND EACH AND ALL BRING SOMETHING DIFFERENT AND UNIQUE

Fashion champions all sorts of characters, from a wide variety of backgrounds, and each and all bring something different and unique. You have to put your trust in Him and have the confidence to find your place and way to be part of this passionate and beautiful world.

OUT OF THE BOAT ... ONTO THE WATER

I prepared to hand in my notice, on returning from holiday, and I was more than a little nervous, especially when my boss innocently asked me "How was your holiday?" I wobbled big time. Change is frightening, yet a real peace came over me as I pressed ahead, and on my last day they laid on a surprise lunch and I was thrilled they were happy for me.

I was aware of Jesus supporting me every step of the way on my journey, and this was just one example of how He oversees every detail of our lives, if we let ourselves see it. I learnt two important lessons that day: God can always be trusted and people can be extremely, and often unexpectedly, gracious. It's us who fear the worst - the foolishness of which was underlined by the sweet card my boss handed to me as I left.

A job shouldn't define us. Sometimes, though, we need to take time to think who we are and what we can offer. I had left without a job to go to... was I mad?

That weekend, at a party someone innocently asked me: "What do you do?" "I've just left a job and am really excited about a new start and new adventure" 'Who was I trying to convince?' I thought to myself, and left the party early, feeling lost and confused.

As I left, I noticed there was a voicemail on my phone from a fashion recruiter; the job on offer wasn't right - but the timing was perfect. At my lowest point, something happened to offer me hope and a confidence that God, whose guidance I so wanted to follow, was right there with me.

GOD, WHOSE GUIDANCE I SO WANTED
TO FOLLOW, WAS RIGHT THERE WITH ME

... AND ONWARDS TO THE HIGH STREET

OVER the coming weeks there were several false starts. Yet, every time I started to despair, something came up. These were stepping stones of faith - growing in me a trust that God really was leading the way.

The next interview was for a three month contract with a high street retailer, I had never worked for a big company, and I thought I had no relevant experience for the role, but they must have liked something about me, because they offered me the job.

I quickly discovered that this brand encapsulated everything I loved; their aesthetic was pretty, vintage, delicate, feminine, detailed and on trend.

This was so like God - Him steering me towards something I had never considered, but was just right for me. He must smile at our so frequent unwillingness to go where He is leading!

At the end of the initial three months, I was offered a full time position and, over the years, this progressed from a junior to senior design role. It was a steep and exciting learning curve, completely different from the fashion world I had experienced.

I went from working on two collections a year, each time culminating at London Fashion Week, into a world where there was a new 'drop' in store every month, with a gradual evolution of several collections throughout the year.

what is the 'purpose' of fashion?

FASHION is to dress and bring out the best in who we want to project - our moods, personalities and identity.

So multiple influences, evolving trends and creating something from this made sense to me.

I get to travel, research and process huge amounts of information into creating our own mood boards and design stories for the brand I work for.

Fashion doesn't need to be elitist, we all wear clothes, we all have our own style, and I loved being part of making this accessible and inspiring.

God doesn't judge us by the label we wear, but by the person we are inside, and I feel very privileged to be a small part of people's wardrobe.

how do you feel about fashion today?

I LONG TO SEE
THE LIFE OF EVERY
PERSON ALONG A
GARMENT'S JOURNEY
BEING BLESSED BY IT

SOCIAL media can make it feel as if fashion, indeed the world, is spinning ever faster and more pressurised. Yet, God helps us to realise we have the power to step away from this and live at the pace we choose.

The question I ask myself is this: how can the fashion we do enhance all the individuals involved – from the crop farmer who grows the cotton through to the spinner, dyer, cutter, sewing machinist, presser, packer, sales assistant ... all the way through to the consumer. Each and everyone matters and I long to see the life of every person along a garment's journey being blessed by it.

FAITH IN THE DAY TO DAY

MY faith is integral to how I work and live, day by day. It guides me in all aspects, to project the voice I want to hear: encouraging, enthusiastic, rejecting swearing and harsh words. My faith also gives me the strength to step back when under pressure and resist knee-jerk reactions, which is often a challenge when everything is so fast-paced. Faith reminds me to be positive and that people must always come first. When travelling to factories there is often time and a change to the cultural setting, which often reveals who people really are, including yourself.

I remember a trip to Mauritius to work with one of the big textile and garment manufacturers, where I would get up early each morning to walk on the beach and spend time with God, asking Him to see me through the day.

One lunchtime everyone was very quiet, and one of the local girls, a softly spoken pattern cutter, revealed she was a singer. Instantly I could imagine her singing 'Amazing Grace' in a church, and later that day, without prompting, she invited to me to come see her singing and as we spoke she told me about her faith as a Christian. The day and the trip were transformed with new purpose and that night, as we worked late, she shared with me how she and her family had been converted from Islam to Christianity as a result of a miraculous healing. I now get an email from her each Christmas, sharing greetings at the time of Jesus' birth.

how do you feel Jesus has been there for you over the years?

I feel quite overwhelmed by how faithful and supportive Jesus has been. Whether it's opening doors I might not open myself, taking away any fear or anxiety, I have sensed His presence and encouragement every step of the way and feel blessed at His giving me the confidence and sense of worth to do what I love.

... a final thought?

WE can all get totally carried away by what we do. But God has kept me grounded. Two of my favourite verses are from Matthew 6:25,28

I tell you, do not worry about your life, what you will eat or drink, or your body, what you will wear ... and why do you worry about your clothes? See how the lilies of the field grow. They do not labour or spin. Yet I tell you that not even Solomon, in all his splendour, was dressed like one of these.

We are told not only to avoid worrying about clothes, but also that God delights in these things as well. I love that.

a bible verse that has empowered your journey?

CAN I have two please?!

the peace of God, which transcends all understanding, will guard your hearts and minds in Christ Jesus
Philippians 4:7

BE STILL AND KNOW THAT I AM GOD *Psalm 46:10*

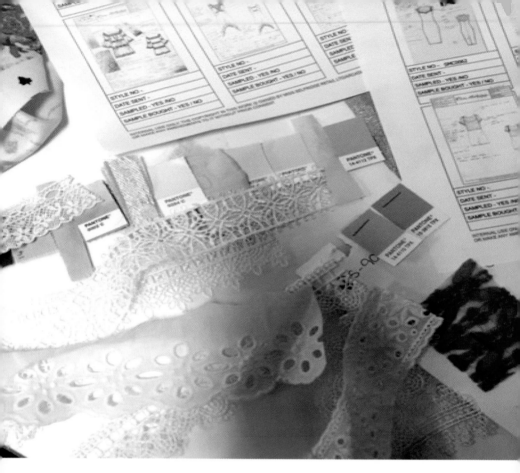

GOD DOESN'T JUDGE US BY THE
LABEL WE WEAR, BUT BY THE
PERSON WE ARE INSIDE, AND I FEEL
VERY PRIVILEGED TO BE A SMALL
PART OF PEOPLE'S WARDROBE

sarah mccowen

A PRAYER FOR
FASHION RETAILERS

THANK YOU LORD, for the beauty
of creation and the constant source of
inspiration You provide throughout
the seasons.

Thank you for all those involved in
the fashion industry across the globe.
Help us all to be kind, encouraging
and inclusive to all, wherever they
live and work, regardless of their
role. May the hands of all that
the product passes through
be blessed and rewarded.

May the clothes we produce bless
and edify those that wear them,
and may it be known in our hearts
that our identity lies not in what
we wear, but in You. Amen

image: Nuru Kimmondo

COURTNEY McCANN

Courtney is a New York based model, working mainly in catalogue and commercial print work. She also does some runway and show rooms, but her favourite are TV commercials. In 2010, she was a Trophy Presenter at the Oscars, carrying the trophies out to the presenters on stage and handing them over as the winner was about to be announced. How was it? AWESOME.

WHATEVER YOU DO
DO IT ALL FOR THE GLORY OF GOD
1 Corinthians 10:31

STARTING OUT ...

courtney's story

I wanted to be a model for a long time. I was tall and shy growing up. My shyness didn't work well in aggressive contact sports like basketball and volleyball, so I ran on the track and got started modelling shortly after high school.

At the time I dreamed that I could be a successful model, but I didn't see how that was possible for me. I never believed I was pretty, or had enough personality. In the beginning, I got into modelling to get out of Bakersfield, my home town. I looked at it as my only opportunity to travel and see places I'd probably never see otherwise. I dabbled in modelling while in college, going to Germany and Paris for a couple of months each, but I returned from each trip to finish school and get a 'real' job. I never had the confidence to see it as a career.

When my dad was suddenly diagnosed with a brain tumor, everything changed. I moved home and enrolled in college in Bakersfield. Shortly afterwards, I got a call from my old manager asking me if I would like to meet with LA Models. I had turned her down so many times before.

I never wanted to be in LA, but now everything was different. I needed distraction, I wanted something different, I wanted escape. So I agreed and started commuting two hours to LA for castings with a full class load. Looking back, it was kind of crazy, and I can't believe I did it. I really didn't think anything would come of it. I didn't think about booking jobs, but eventually I did and a year and a half later I graduated from college and didn't need to look for a job. I had one, doing modelling, and it was going well. That was 2007 and I've been working ever since.

image: Jason Lowrie

MY FIRST BIG RUNWAY SHOW

FIVE months after after I started commuting for castings in LA, I got booked on a four day runway job in Las Vegas. I was excited because this job paid more than I had ever been paid. It wasn't very much, but it was a lot to me then as a college student. It was also the job that allowed me to quit working at the restaurant in Bakersfield.

It was also my first time in Las Vegas. The Vegas part wasn't that exciting to me, but I was thrilled to be booked on this job. All the other models in the show were experienced and confident. Each day we had two shows, one in the morning and one in the evening. I was so nervous and I wondered if anyone could tell (they could!).

The first night, my agent called me at the hotel and she asked me how it was going. She gave me some pointers and words of encouragement to build me up.

I was a little embarrassed at the time because I think the client complained, but her words were so gentle and encouraging. She really believed in me and gave me a chance. That moment was a milestone, because I realised I could trust her.

Having been in the industry for a while, I now see how much God blessed me and protected me by giving me such a good agent, especially in such a brutal industry.

I NOW SEE HOW MUCH GOD
BLESSED ME AND PROTECTED ME

great things about working in fashion

IT'S fun, creative, playful. Its not rocket science and unfortunately it doesn't save lives, but it doesn't have to, either. It's art, its collaborating, its always changing (or being resurrected over and over), it's fleeting. As a model, I've got to see how much work goes in to designing collections that are trying to predict what the trends will be, and what people will want to buy two to three seasons ahead of time.

TRAVELLING the world. Modelling was always my way to adventure in life. I never used to think I'd be able to go many places in life on my own accomplishments, and I looked at modelling as an opportunity to have adventure and see a life I'd never otherwise get to see. Fashion cities are some of the most exciting on the Earth and, if you want, a model can go anywhere and get an agency and live there for a while. It's a pretty unique job.

I HAVE enjoyed working with clients behind the scenes. I have been a fit model in production meetings for different brands, feeling like a fly on the wall hearing all the inner workings of the company and learning the design process and all of the work, detail, hours, and creativity that goes into the process. I've learned a lot about how fashion companies make their clothes and have to market them to sell. No matter how big the brand, its still such a personal process for the people involved, and I have enjoyed being able to experience and help in that process.

challenges you face as a model?

THE challenging part of being a model is tied to the rewarding part! It's great to have such flexibility in my schedule and work, but there is no guarantee of employment. Every job could potentially be the last time a client will hire you. There isn't a lot of consistency and, if there is, it will only be for a few seasons.

There are so many models and there is so much competition. At the end of the day, we are very replaceable. Clients have their favourites but, if they need to, they can and will find someone else. I'm learning the balance of choosing when to take a job and when to rest, and to be thankful for the jobs I do get, not becoming too 'big' to do a 'small' job.

I have to let go of the fact that nothing is personal, and my body doesn't dictate my worth, and neither does my level of busyness. God has taught me a lot and is still teaching me where to find my security and value. It's always and only in Him.

MY BODY
DOESN'T
DICTATE
MY WORTH

GOD IS STILL
TEACHING ME
WHERE TO FIND
MY SECURITY
AND VALUE

image: Nuru Kimmondo

how does your faith help you in the day to day?

KNOWING Christ is everything. At the end
of the day, I can lay my head down knowing
that all my efforts are nothing without Christ,
and ultimately God is faithful, no matter what.

Being a Christian helps me trust that, however
I feel about how my castings or the job went
- whether I get rejection or praise from
clients - it is all in God's control.

Trusting God with my life helps me know
He will provide jobs, when I don't think I will
work. It helps me know that I am enough,
even when I get rejected. It helps me find
purpose, when many people don't take models
seriously. It helps me let go of comparing and
competition on the job, enabling me to give
and share with the other models I meet.

God's love and wisdom has protected me from
making terrible decisions and compromising
my body and integrity for the sake of 'art'
and 'getting ahead'.

TRUSTING GOD
HELPS ME KNOW
THAT I AM
ENOUGH EVEN
WHEN I GET
REJECTED

*I consider everything
a loss compared to the
surpassing greatness of
knowing Christ Jesus
my Lord* Philippians 3:8

have you always been so secure in your faith?

MY mom recently reminded me of something I said when I was
fifteen years old. I asked her if it was ungodly to model. She told
me it depended on what you do with it. I replied: "If I ever
become a model, I will tell girls about Jesus."

In the beginning of my career, I wasn't walking with Jesus. I knew
Him and was saved, but never understood what it meant to have a
relationship with Jesus and living in grace. I just prayed when I was
scared, but I didn't really trust my life over to the Lord. That said,
I think it's very interesting that I said that to my mom, as now I'm
actually living it out. It encourages me that, when God starts a work
in you, He doesn't stop. Even though I detoured away from God for
more than a few years, Jesus never stopped loving and pursuing me.

GOD'S PLAN ... OUR DESIRES?

TRAVELLING to London in 2014 for the first time was a milestone for me, because it showed me how much God loves and cares about what we desire.

I'd always wanted to go to London. I just didn't think I could go for work. I thought I was too old to travel to a new market and didn't think I was 'allowed' to go somewhere just because I wanted to!

It started when I saw the movie 'About Time'. It's a great film, which takes place in London, and I walked out of the theatre wishing I could go on a trip there. My best friend encouraged me to go and get an agency. I thought I was too 'old' to do the travelling model thing, but couldn't get the idea out of my head. I decided to pray about it and asked God to open doors for agency and accommodation - if it was good.

Within a couple months, an agency was offering me jobs, a free place to stay in Greenwich and I had friends I already knew in London. Since then, God has continued to bless me with jobs there. I really love that city and keep praying God will open doors for me to be in London for modelling and beyond, whatever His purposes may be.

That first trip to London was just so special, because God gave me so many little gifts that I know only he could have tailor made for me. It really changed my life, to dream big and open up to the possibilities with God.

IT REALLY CHANGED MY LIFE,
TO DREAM BIG AND OPEN UP
TO THE POSSIBILITIES WITH GOD

what do you know now that you wish you knew when you started out?

I wish I had more confidence in myself and my personality. I was always trying to be exactly who I thought people wanted me to be. When you do that, you end up being nobody. Authenticity is liberating for everyone - the individual and the people around them - and it usually comes with confidence, or at least it comes across that way. I wish I had known I could be myself.

what advice would you give to someone at the start of their career?

I would advise they should view modelling as a temporary job, and also work on something else. It's a career for some people, but the longevity for most is to mid-thirties and, by then, even if you are still successful, it's not a career that is very satisfying to someone at that age in life.

It's hard to wake up and realise you want to do more, use your mind and creativity in a work field, yet all you feel you know how to do is 'model'. I am thankful to have a Bachelors Degree in Business-Marketing, but I wish I would have spent more time discovering other passions and really looked into what work I can do after modelling. When the only job you've done for eight years is modelling, it begins to feel like that's all I can do.

I'm going through that process now and I'm excited to see what God reveals and provides. In the meantime, I'm so thankful for the jobs I have. For all I know, God may have me continue modelling for a while, but using it as the 'fundraiser' for the real work He wants me to invest and focus on. I suppose this is the purpose for everyone's career.

image: Nuru Kimmondo

are you a workaholic?

I am a workaholic ... or was. A lot has changed for me in the last year. God has opened my eyes to why I was really striving after modelling, and to see how much I found my identity in work and whether I was successful.

I have been actively trying to take more time off work to invest my time and energy in other things. I've discovered more about myself and been able to detach from Courtney the model, and just be me.

I WISH I HAD KNOWN
I COULD BE MYSELF

what would you say to those who assert that fashion is no place for a Christian?

EVEN though the need for clothing is technically because of sin, God still works it for good. He gave man the genius to make beautiful fashion out of the materials of the earth ... clothing that is beautiful, soft, luxurious, warm, comfortable, colourful, expressive, fun ... the possibilities are endless because God's is infinite in His creative genius!

Do not worry how you will defend yourself or what you will say, for the Holy Spirit will teach you at that time what you should say Luke 12:11,12

ever said anything daft as you've tried to be salt and light?

HA!!! So many times! For me it usually comes out when I'm discussing my values and feeling I have to defend them.

Afterwards, as I'm beating myself up for not saying the right thing, God humbles me with His love and shows me the fruit is not in what I say, but how I treat the person afterwards.

I find that non-believers feel judged when they hear truth ... naturally. God has show me that I need to keep loving and seeking to know and care for the person I've just disagreed with, even if it's awkward. Just because we don't agree doesn't mean I stop trying to engage and love. That has been a very rewarding lesson God recently taught me.

has your faith sometimes made a difference to the decisions you have taken?

I have declined jobs because they compromised the contracts and commitments I have with my agents. Even when no one would find out, I know God called me to honour my commitments and be honest. I also don't model lingerie. It's something God put on my heart for me to be faithful in.

I know God calls each of us to do different things depending on the grace He's given us for His purposes and to be faithful to what God calls YOU to and you alone.

God's top commandment for your work in fashion?

Teach me Your way, Lord, that I may rely on Your faithfulness; give me an undivided heart Psalm 86:11

I'M learning that to be a Christian and follow Jesus means that nothing is separate from Him. Our lives don't have compartments. I made allowances for my Model-self and Christian-self, forgetting that I am in Christ - ALL of me. When I compartmentalise my Christian walk, it creates confusion, which leads to doubt, and ultimately diminishes what God can do through my life. It takes God away from being at the top and makes an idol out of modelling.

image: Nuru Kimmondo

BEING A CHRISTIAN MAKES
MODELLING SO MUCH MORE
COMPLICATED, BECAUSE THERE
ARE MANY JOBS I WON'T DO AND
FASHIONS I WON'T WEAR, WHICH
POTENTIALLY TAKES ME OUT OF A
LOT OF JOBS. I'VE LEARNED I NEED
TO COMMUNICATE MY BOUNDARIES
RESPECTFULLY AND OPENLY.
WHEN I DO THIS, IT MAKES LIFE
SO MUCH MORE SIMPLE. I KNOW
WHERE I STAND AND SO DO
THE PEOPLE I WORK WITH

courtney mccann

A PRAYER FOR
FASHION MODELS

FATHER GOD, we lift before you
models, boys and girls, working in
studios, showrooms and on catwalks
around the world. Enable all to respect
the value of their work, not just as
hangers for the clothes they model,
but as artists working with the
designers and their teams, to convey
beauty and the power of the clothes to
inspire live audiences, photographers
and the media consumer. Grant them
courage to model only what their
consciences are comfortable with.

Keep models safe, not just physically,
as they travel to new cities and far out
places for castings and fittings, but
in their sense of self worth. We pray
against those who would exploit or
abuse them. Multiply the initiatives that
work for their nurture and protection.

We ask for Your blessing on
Models for Christ, working with
models around the world to stand
by them and facilitate community
service projects. Amen

NATASHA RUFUS ISAACS & LAVINIA BRENNAN

Beulah London is a luxury fashion brand founded by Natasha Rufus Isaacs and Lavinia Brennan. It is based on British design, heritage and the empowerment of women. Beulah has gained international acclaim as a luxury fashion brand with a social conscience, which has inspired some of the world's most influential women to wear the label.

A LOVE OF FASHION
A HEART FOR SOCIAL JUSTICE

beulahlondon.com

FOUNDATIONS & EARLY INFLUENCES

*lavinia &
natasha's story*

LAVINIA: I was born and schooled in London. After a gap year 'following the sun' in South East Asia and the Pacific, I studied History of Art & Theology at the University of Durham.

On graduating, I had no real idea of what to do next except that, after doing some internships in fashion PR, I was drawn towards fashion. My grandmother was a big style icon for me - she was such an elegant dresser, and worked with a tailor to make sure her Bruce Oldfield, Hardy Amies and Jean Muir dresses fitted just right.

I was strongly influenced by this, and the fact that both she and my mother were artists. I was no good at the practical aspects, though; it was the background to paintings, the economics and politics of the day, that had attracted me. And then, my mother had such a servant heart; she was always mentoring young, single mothers and fostering children. When I came back from university at holiday times, I found I had to share my mum's bed, as there were foster children in all the other rooms!

NATASHA: Brought up in Gloucestershire, my family background is rich in variety, ranging from a chemist and zoologist, to an artist and the boxing champion of England - in the 1790s! My father (Fourth Marquess of Reading), was always an inspiration. He has no social qualms, and can talk as easily to a homeless person on the Tube, as he can to the Prime Minister. And then my great-great-grandfather was Viceroy of India in the 1920s, and was passionate about driving India towards reform and self-governance.

Like Lavinia, I studied History of Art and, looking back, and unlikely as it might seem, I can see how all this was paving the way for Beulah.

*what is the glue that holds
your partnership together?*

BOTH: Our grandmothers were (are)
best friends, so we knew each other from
when we were young. We were Christians
from an early age and were part of Holy
Trinity Brompton, the home of Alpha
and much else. Family and faith were the
foundations of our friendship, so it sort
of seemed natural when we decided to
start a business together.

*where did faith fit in as you
started out?*

NATASHA: I think we both wrestled with
our faith. As a teenager you start to wonder
whether it's real or whether it's all a result of
what your parents have taught you. But, over
time, I think we each grew out of that and
really found our own faith. An intense time
in India brought us closer to those beliefs
and, as a result, we often stop to pray out
loud together in the office or just before
we go into meetings. During times of real
difficulty with the company, praying together
has got us through some sticky patches.

LAVINIA: My mum started working for the
church when I was thirteen, and I was part
of a good group of friends there. But my faith
was heavily reliant on my mum, the friends
and the church. I had not considered it in
detail. When Nats and I first went to India
I found that my faith was tied up with my
heart, not just an intellectual understanding.
I discovered that God's broken my heart
for what breaks His.

GOD'S BROKEN MY HEART FOR WHAT BREAKS HIS

A LIFE CHANGING TRIP

I FELT STRANGELY AT
HOME HELPING THE
BOYS AND GIRLS WHO
HAD SUFFERED MUCH

I HAD THIS IDEA
OF SETTING UP
A SHOE BUSINESS
AND INVOLVING THE
WOMEN TO PROVIDE
THEM WITH INCOME
IN PLACE OF WHAT
THEY EARNED ON
THE STREETS

NATASHA: After university, I worked at Sotheby's for a while and then, in 2007, left to help out at Holy Trinity Brompton, my home church, where I organised projects for the homeless and arranged prison visits for volunteers. A good friend at HTB had been in India for six months, working in a home supporting girls rescued from the sex trade. Lavs and I decided we should go, too. And so it was, in 2009, that we found ourselves boarding a plane to India, to work in Atulya, an aftercare home in the Delhi slums.

LAVINIA: In the mornings, Nats taught at a local slum school and I helped to home-school six boys born with HIV. In the afternoon, we came together at the care home, helping in a workshop, where the girls made lavender bags.

Weirdly enough, I felt strangely at home helping the boys and girls who had suffered much. It was my daily commute through the Delhi traffic that phased me most. And it was not just the noise and bustle, but the learing eyes and the lust for women that was so ghastly. No wonder sex trafficking is such a huge problem.

NATASHA: As we got a feel for things, I had this idea of setting up a shoe business and involving the women to provide them with income in place of what they earned on the streets. We approached a couple of factories, but the doors were closed (because we were women?) So, instead, we started talking about making dresses, and got in touch with a lady at a factory that manufactured for the London-based designers Jenny Packham and Matthew Williamson.

LAVINIA: What did we think we were doing? We were completely naive and it was complete madness. And why did she say yes? I've no idea. She may have thought: English girls = $$$$$! ... or, God may have been having some fun helping us get started! Whatever. We came away with ten really expensive samples.

sounds like you had a charmed start to your business?

LAVINIA: It's been a real roller-coaster. We have indeed been fortunate with the support we received from family and friends, with the publicity that came with high profile clients, and the fact that God seemed to open doors that really shouldn't have opened quite so quickly. Selling in Harvey Nichols and Fenwicks within a couple of seasons was a dream.

Yet, the day to day struggles of growing a young business are very real: identifying core customers and an aesthetic that works for them and us; getting pricing architecture right; premises, sampling, accounts, cash flow. We're even having to review our name as there is a company, 'Beulah Style' in the US, which is an important market for us.

We firmly believe we are following a path that God is leading us down, but that doesn't mean we don't have to grapple with the daily challenges that all businesses face.

how real is your faith in the day to day running of Beulah?

NATASHA: Faith is a very present reality through each day. Dotted around our studios we have reminders: 'Believe in miracles'; 'Live by the trinity of what is true, good and beautiful'; and written into the stitching of many of our clothes are phrases like: 'Love like you've never been hurt, dance as though no one is watching, sing as though no one can hear you'. We regularly pray about decisions to be taken and challenges to be overcome. Our faith is a thread running through all we do.

where does the name 'Beulah' come from?

No longer will they call you Deserted, or name your land Desolate. But you will be called Hephzibah (meaning: my delight is in her) and your land Beulah (married), for the Lord will take delight in you and your land will be married. Isaiah 62:4

... and your inspiration?

The Spirit of the Sovereign Lord is on me, because the Lord has anointed me to preach good news to the poor. He has sent me to bind up the broken hearted, to proclaim freedom to the captives, and release from darkness for the prisoners .... Isaiah 61:1

FOR EACH BEAUTIFUL GARMENT WE MAKE THERE IS AN EQUALLY BEAUTIFUL CHANGE HAPPENING SOMEWHERE IN THE WORLD

BEULAH LONDON...

AMAZING GRACE!
HOW SWEET THE
SOUND THAT SAVED
A WRETCH LIKE ME.
I ONCE WAS LOST
BUT NOW AM FOUND
WAS BLIND BUT
NOW I SEE
John Newton

LAVINIA: Back in the UK, I asked my mum if we could set up shop in her living room. Another "yes". What an amazing woman she is! A year later we moved into The Old Gas Works, off the Kings Road, which offers affordable studios and offices to a community of 300 individuals and organisations across the creative industries and supporting businesses.

NATASHA: Our first collection was entitled Amazing Grace, which resonated with the much loved hymn written in 1779 by the former slave trader, John Newton. The dresses were worn by the rich and famous. But it was Indian women, who had once lived disease-ridden lives and faced the prospect of premature deaths, who helped bring them to life. I just love that juxtaposition - luxury and beauty supporting social justice.

We had also heard about Freeset, the Fairtrade business offering employment and salaries to women previously trapped in Kolkata's sex ring, and it seemed ideal to support it.

LAVINIA: We design the clothes in London, have a sample mocked up, then send it out to Delhi, where girls who are fairly paid by the government-protected scheme, make the dresses. The Kolkata based women are not yet sufficiently skilled to do this, so they create our canvas bags, which we give to customers with every purchase.

Our aim was to show the women that alternative and sustainable livelihoods exist, and the results were heartening. Women choosing to be busy in a life without depravity and demeaning behaviour, had the opportunity to work for our brand, once they arrive at the two shelters in Delhi and Kolkata.

THE BEULAH TRUST...

beulahlondon.com/the-beulah-trust

THE Beulah Trust was founded in January 2013 to put our humanitarian mission into action, with a clear goal of supporting projects and initiatives that create sustainable livelihoods for victims of trafficking. The Trust aims to give grants that pay for skill courses giving women who have been victims of sex trafficking and abuse the chance to find work, generate an income, and live a self-sufficient life, free from abuse. The Beulah Trust is the heart of what Beulah is about and, as Beulah grows, we hope to make a real difference to the lives of women who have been trafficked.

OUR CHARITABLE VISION is to contribute towards eradicating modern day slavery. We want to be an inspirational voice for a new generation, proclaiming that a woman's freedom is not a luxury. We see a world where freedom is expected and where slavery no longer exists. The Beulah Trust will act as a bridge supporting chosen charities to provide women who have been trafficked or are vulnerable to being trafficked with a chance to build a new life, free from abuse.

EMPLOYMENT We aim to create more job opportunities as the company grows and volumes increase. Currently, we are working with a fairtrade business, Freeset, which offers employment to women trapped in Kolkata's sex trade. Freeset is dedicated to helping trafficked women and women who are regarded as high risk of ending up in the sex trade, by providing them with a steady income, a bank account and chance to build a new life free from abuse. In the last few years, Freeset have employed a further fifty women, breaking the cycle of poverty in the most marginalised communities. Revenue from sales of our bags goes to support this.

PARTNERSHIPS

Since 2011, Beulah has supported the United Nations' 'Blue Heart Campaign', which raises awareness of the issue of human trafficking and funds for its victims. We donate 10% of profits from our blue heart scarf and blue heart shawl to the campaign. Through our partnership with the 'Blue Heart Campaign', we aim to inspire other brands to join in the fight against human trafficking by collaborating to create more blue heart products. In 2013, we launched our blue heart pump in partnership with French Sole.

FREEDOM SHOULD NEVER BE A LUXURY

EDUCATION

Through the Trust, we seek to support women through third parties (UK & International) for the advancement of education and training, and providing support designed to enable individuals to generate a sustainable income and become self-sufficient.

DO NOT CONFORM ANY LONGER TO THE PATTERN OF THIS WORLD, BUT BE TRANSFORMED BY THE RENEWING OF YOUR MIND
Romans 12:2

image: Katrina Lawson Johnston

FASHION CAN'T LIVE
IN ISOLATION FROM
THE REAL WORLD

Image: Katrina Lawson Johnston

DREAMS FOR THE FUTURE

LAVINIA: Our dream is to go beyond fashion into a luxury lifestyle brand with a strong focus to 'do good and be a voice for change'. This is going back to our original vision, stimulating a movement of people combining beautiful things with social justice. We want to help people look at fashion differently, rather than simply conforming to the pressure for a continual stream of new collections.

We see ourselves as something of a laboratory for ideas and principals that redefine what 'success' means, helping people to realise that fashion can't live in isolation from the real world. Rather, it has the opportunity to link together the consumer with those who produce what they buy in a meaningful and transformational way.

We would love other businesses to consider adopting something similar to ten key factors that are at the core of what we aim to do, and how we want to do it - as follows:

SUCCESS FOR US IS NOT THE SIZE OF TURNOVER OR MEDIA COVERAGE; RATHER THE NUMBER OF LIVES TRANSFORMED BY OUR BUSINESS

a bible verse that has empowered your journey?

I KNOW THE PLANS I HAVE FOR YOU, DECLARES THE LORD, PLANS TO PROSPER YOU AND NOT TO HARM YOU, PLANS TO GIVE YOU HOPE AND A FUTURE
Jeremiah 29:11

1. Our vision is for 80% of our collection to be touched by the women who have escaped trafficking - whether it be by them making the entirety of the piece, a trim or the lining.

2. 10% (a biblical tithe) of our gross profit, once we have raised investment, will go back to the Beulah Trust.

3. We try not to work at weekends, otherwise we become less productive.

4. Regularly reading about current affairs is as important to us as the latest edition of Vogue.

5. We want to break the mould of having to continually create new for the sake of new.

6. We aim to work in partnership with others to create fresh perspective on all we do.

7. We will pass on to others what we have learned, as part of a healthy growth strategy.

8. Success, for us, is not the size of turnover or media coverage; rather the number of lives transformed by our business.

9. We want to be an inspirational voice for a new generation, proclaiming that a woman's freedom is not a luxury.

10. Our hearts' desire: to change the world, not be conformed by it.

OUR HEARTS' DESIRE:
TO CHANGE THE WORLD
NOT BE CONFORMED BY IT

natasha rufus isaacs
& lavinia brennan

A PRAYER FOR
FASHION'S POTENTIAL
TO CREATE NEW HOPE

FATHER GOD, You call us, not to be
conformed to the pattern of the world,
but to allow our minds to be opened,
so that we might transform the way
the world works.

Grant energy and success to those
businesses which seek to follow the ways
revealed in Your Word, and give them
continuing courage to pursue their plans,
even when times are challenging from a
purely business perspective, trusting that
where You lead, You will provide.

May a growing number of fashion
businesses have the vision and
determination to operate in a way
that honours You, brings hope to
those in need around the world,
and makes the best use of the talents
of the people working for them. Amen

FAITH - FEMINISM - FASHION

RUTH AWOGBADE

Ruth studied politics at Durham University, starting shortly after she had suffered a triple family bereavement. Having space to review her faith and life priorities, she launched MAGNIFY at the age of nineteen. One of Ruth's visions is to prove to women that Christianity can be integrated with their lives as females and their passions.

image: MAGNIFY Magazine - Mattias Bjorklund

hellomagnify.com

MAGNIFY ... THE STORY SO FAR

MAGNIFY is a dream I wake up to everyday - and I would never change that. Martin Luther King's quote that: "faith is taking the first step even when you don't see the full staircase" is an apt description of the journey over the last few years.

I started MAGNIFY in February 2008, aged nineteen, in my first year at Durham University. The vision was born out of a personal experience, when through a series of life challenges, my faith was really shaken. In hindsight, I've come to believe that everything happens for a reason. As trying as that time was, it gave me the opportunity to wrestle with my faith and explore my doubts. It ultimately led me to find out what Christianity meant for me, and I consequently started a personal relationship with Jesus that changed my life.

The vision of MAGNIFY has always been to give women the chance to explore the Christian faith in an unpressured, engaging and creative way, how it can impact being a woman in today's world. As a team, we're passionate about creating a platform that gives us as women the chance to bring to the table our strengths, weaknesses, fears and vulnerabilities - with no judgement.

'Faith, Feminism and Fashion - The Christian Women's Magazine breaking every stereotype' is how the Huffington Post described us just a few weeks after the launch of our inaugural issue. Such a description was humbling, to say the least. We hope our content speaks to the real issues that women are facing, and through a beautifully conveyed aesthetic, presents them in a way that will be relevant for generations to come.

MAGNIFY

- says every woman has a unique identity and purpose
- creates discussions around faith, feminism and fashion and their impact on our day to day lives through our print magazine, digital content and events
- is a catalyst for community; a showcase for cutting-edge style; through intriguing interviews and dynamic articles

WHERE DID THE NAME "MAGNIFY" COME FROM?

AFTER weeks of brainstorming, the vision didn't have a name. Then one day in Spring 2008, I was walking into a newsagent in Durham and the name 'MAGNIFY' suddenly came to me. The Bible verse I attribute it to is Mary's outburst of praise when she learns that will be giving birth to the Messiah: "My soul doth magnify the Lord" (Luke 1:46 - King James Version)

At the time, I was also reading a book called 'Desiring God', by an American preacher, John Piper. In the book, he explained the idea that when we use our lives and talents to bring glory to (magnify) God, is when our lives can truly be fulfilled.

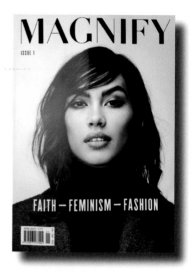

... AND THE STRAPLINE: 'FAITH - FEMINISM - FASHION'?

TRYING to descibe the vision I had for MAGNIFY was difficult to explain. I said to God: "This is really stressful." Yet, I didn't want to be smart and come up with something like an advertising slogan, so I decided to leave the idea of a tagline to one side. However, one day soon after, I'd just walked into Sainsbury's (a shop again!), and it suddenly came into my head: 'Faith - Feminism - Fashion'. The words perfectly captured what I was trying to say. I take no credit for it!

FAITH is the foundation of why we started and why we exist. As a team we each have a personal relationship with Jesus that has changed our lives so we want to share His love with others.

FEMINISM means we celebrate women.

FASHION is visually how we tell stories.

DO CHURCHES HAVE A PARTICULAR PROBLEM WITH FEMINISM?

I often think that churches (whose leadership is usually male-dominated) can find it a challenge to encourage women, without putting them in a box or stereotyping our expectations of life. Often the view of inspiring women is limited to teaching them to aspire to be a 'perfect wife'. Although for many of us that will be an important role to fulfil, I think it's important that women's gifts and talents are nurtured as celebrated just as with men.

WHAT DOES 'FEMINISM' MEAN TO YOU? Simply believing that men and women are equal, albeit different. With everything in life there are various extreme expressions, but I am not someone who views everything through a 'feminist' lens.

WHAT DO YOU MAKE OF ST PAUL'S INSTRUCTION THAT:
'Women should remain silent in the churches'?

IN A CULTURE WHERE THEY WERE OFTEN NOT SEEN AS EQUAL, THE TIME JESUS SPENT WITH WOMEN, AT CRITICAL POINTS, SHOWED THE VALUE HE PLACED ON THEM

ONE woman I spoke to told me her church is 70% women, but there were never any women up front, and it was really hard to relate to all male leadership, all the time.

Whilst it is not easy to challenge verses quoted at you, I can't see that it is right that women are simply seen but not heard. And then some women have the sense that they can't start doing things within the church until they get married. What happens if you don't get married?

WOMEN AS BISHOPS?

NOT a problem for me, as I'm not planning to become one! Seriously, I do think we get so hung up on things, when our priority should be to share the love of God. It is desperately needed by so many people.

JESUS SEEMED TO HAVE SPENT A LOT OF TIME WITH WOMEN - WHY DO YOU THINK HE DID?

JESUS was radical in the way he displayed His love for people - often defying social conventions. There are many examples, but it is telling, for instance, that the first person to see Him after the resurrection was a woman. In a culture where they were often not seen as equal, the time Jesus spent with women at critical points showed the value He placed on them.

HOW DOES FASHION HELP WOMEN CONNECT THEIR FAITH WITH CELEBRATING WHO THEY ARE?

IN Genesis, we see God as the ultimate Creator. Even the fact that the Bible, as a book recording stories of people's lives, shows how God planned to be the guiding framework of our lives, reveals the artistry of God. Fashion is a way to express ourselves as human beings and impacts our day to day lives. I think there is a parallel with how a personal faith relationship is a way we express ourselves.

MAGNIFY, ISSUE 1 CARRIED AN ARTICLE CHALLENGING TRADITIONAL VIEWS OF BEAUTY. HOW DO YOU SEE THIS?

AS a black woman growing up, through media, I often only saw a singular presentation of beauty. As a team, we are extremely diverse from many different backgrounds so, through MAGNIFY, we want to authentically present that beauty can be found in all people - not just through their appearance, but their strength, their stories and their character.

image: MAGNIFY Magazine - André Wagner

WE GET SO HUNG UP ON THINGS,
WHEN OUR PRIORITY SHOULD BE
TO SHARE THE LOVE OF GOD.
IT IS DESPERATELY NEEDED
BY SO MANY PEOPLE

ruth awogbade

A PRAYER FOR
FAITH, FEMINISM & FASHION

FATHER GOD

We believe that, as humans, we have all
been created with a unique identity, and
have all been blessed with incredible
talents to use for our own good and
for the benefit of others.

Please show favour to MAGNIFY, that it
might be a platform that connects women
- both to their Creator and to each other.

May MAGNIFY inspire every day women
to dream, and to create a future that they
wish to see.

May this generation and those to come, by
using creativity, go on to make a difference
in every sphere of influence.

Amen

KATRINA
LAWSON JOHNSTON

Katrina is an emerging
London- based freelance
photographer. A graduate of the
London College of Fashion, she
started out as a Studio Assistant
at Spring Studios and then as
Studio Manager for Jacob Sutton.

MY TUTOR ANNOUNCED
THAT THIS WAS MY BEST
WORK TO DATE. "REALLY?
IT'S JUST A FEW IMAGES
OF AN OLD LADY!"
"YOU'RE WRONG,"
HE REPLIED, "YOU'RE
FINDING YOUR VOICE."

katrinalawsonjohnston.com

AN UNCONVENTIONAL START

I was a competitive ice skater until I was twenty, reaching no. 5 in the UK. When it became apparent, though, that this was as far as I could go on the ice, rather than turn to coaching or taking part in show skating, I decided to move on.

katrina's story

image: Chris Moore

I'd had a little insight into the fashion industry: when I was fifteen, I had the amazing and extra-ordinary experience of walking for McQueen: he wanted ice skaters for his AW'99 show 'The Overlook', so I went for the casting and had a fitting with him. I was completely in awe of the creations his team where making and that started the excitement for fashion. I would often scour my dad's newspaper for Hilary Alexander's fashion pages and occasionally persuade him to buy me Vogue or Harpers Bazaar.

Nevertheless, it was something of an unknown world that I found myself in when I enrolled at the London College of Fashion to study a BA in fashion photography.

My mother was a significant influence too. She was a keen amateur photographer and particularly loved shooting flora - she'd tidy the grass away and photograph the rare wild flowers on our walking holidays in the mountains. It was fascinating to watch her and I was delighted when, aged sixteen, I was given my first camera, a Nikon FM2.

THE BUSY AND FAST
PACE OF LONDON
EXCITED AND
INSPIRED ME,
I LOVED IT

I found myself attracted towards fine art photography but, when I came to seriously consider a future career, I decided that the larger and more commercial world of fashion would be a much better bet.

So, when I moved up to London, I was very excited at the prospect of studying in the midst of one of the world's greatest cities for fashion, art and culture. The busy and fast pace of London excited and inspired me, I loved it.

111

how did faith play out in your formative years?

MY grandfather had a massive conversion experience in the 1970s, his Christian faith becoming a major part of his life. So it wasn't surprising that I inherited a learned faith, which I took on board pretty much as I was told it. But when I moved away from home to London to study and embraced my new-found independence, I may have continued to call myself a Christian, but I wasn't living it.

When a relationship ended with my then boyfriend, it was really nasty and I slipped into clinical depression. I was determined not to resort to medication, but tackle it through therapy. A key part of my recuperation was two friends who came alongside; one a Christian, one not. There was real power in this group of three and we are still close to this day.

Having dealt with all this, and whilst throwing myself into my studies, I was soon to be shaken up, when a Buddhist tutor showed the class an Andres Serrano image of a plastic crucifix in a jar of golden liquid. He then announced that it was entitled "Piss Christ", for the liquid was urine. No one else in the class appeared to bat an eyelid. I felt physically sick. So, my faith wasn't so dormant.

I reckon God was on my case, as this coincided with my coming into contact with a new friend working in the industry as a make-up artist. Isabelle was a Christian and I couldn't believe that someone who had the same creative interests could live out her faith in the industry - everything with her seemed to be in harmony and that was very attractive.

Isabelle showed a real interest in me and answered lots of my searching questions. She introduced me to Alpha (a free course which explores the big questions regarding the Christian faith) and also a lively church full of people my age. Church has become a key part of my faith and a highlight of my week.

a cultural obsession with the young

CONTEMPORARY culture is obsessed with youth. Particularly within women's fashion, it is a rarity when someone from an older generation is celebrated. The Bible clearly teaches us to honour our parents (Exodus 20:12) and the older generation (Leviticus 19:32). I found out that creatively I have a particular heart for photographing older women. The people I have photographed are inspiring, strong women with amazing wisdom and strength. I feel I can learn so much from those who have seen more of life then me, and I want to honour them in the only way I know how; through photography.

SHOW RESPECT FOR
THE ELDERLY AND
REVERE YOUR GOD
Leviticus 19:32

image: Katrina Lawson Johnston

OPPORTUNITIES AT UNIVERSITY

AT the London College of Fashion, I felt like I had started my life for real. In such a stimulating environment, I began to learn to think for myself, to expand my mind, to hold opinions.

A key moment came as I was heading into my final year: my tutor advised me to "stop trying to do the right thing (in my work) and go and do what you love". So I went up to Northumberland to shoot my granny. We have a great relationship and she has an incredible mind. She is a real source of inspiration for life to me and it seemed a natural thing to do.

I worked on a composite portrait, trying to capture all the aspects that made her who she was to me through a series of photographs. When I presented this work to my tutor he announced that this was my best work to date. "Really? It's just a few images of an older lady!" "You're wrong," he replied, "it's valid, you're finding your voice." This encouragement led me to explore the idea of memory and identity through the use of photographs, particularly in fashion advertising.

I was starting to learn what my creative style was, what interested me and to grow the confidence to go with it. Even today, I am still on a journey, searching for an ever clearer picture of what makes me tick creatively, becoming more confident to go with what I would intuitively do, rather than wondering what and how I 'ought' to shoot.

But those weeks with granny, and the encouraging feedback, I received kick started my career as I went on to focus on celebrating (usually ignored) older women in a lot of my early work.

I BEGAN TO LEARN
TO THINK FOR MYSELF
TO EXPAND MY MIND
TO HOLD OPINIONS

image: Katrina Lawson Johnston

I AM STILL
ON A JOURNEY
SEARCHING FOR
AN EVER CLEARER
PICTURE OF WHAT
MAKES ME TICK
CREATIVELY

INTO THE WORKPLACE

TWO THINGS
I HAD LEARNED
AS A SKATER ...
DETERMINATION
& DISCIPLINE

TWO things I had learned as a skater were determination and discipline; I had worked out a plan and was fortunate enough to go straight into work at Spring Studios in North London as a studio assistant. There was no shortage of menial tasks; I was learning all about the kit, the processes, the people and I was being paid for it. I made it my mission to get to know as many other assistants and shoot producers as I could, for I'd worked out that a key to getting on in fashion was to have a great network.

After six months I moved to being a freelance assistant, working for half a dozen or so photographers in London and travelling to Europe with a few of them, all the contacts for which had come through my networking at Spring. It was a great experience and helped me to work out whom I wanted to work for in the long-term.

At this stage, my faith was developing quickly and I found myself questioning what I was doing and why. 'Is it OK to be in fashion?' After a year freelancing I was offered a full time position with a leading London photographer and film maker called Jacob Sutton. Although at the same time I was toying with the idea of moving to Paris to work for another big-time photographer who had offered me a full time position, it felt so right to take the job with Jacob, so I did.

I FOUND MYSELF
QUESTIONING
WHAT I WAS
DOING AND WHY:
'IS IT OK TO BE
IN FASHION?'

I was his studio manager and, alongside a lot of admin working with his producer and agency, I was on set with the other assistants looking after the kit and seeing how he looked at things and how he developed his ideas. It was a fascinating time and I absolutely loved my job and the people.

Jacob is an artist working in a fashion environment - a real visionary. I learned so much from him and feel that my time spent in his employment gave me a much greater understanding of all aspects of being a photographer than perhaps any other job opportunity would have taught.

Both he and many of those I worked with there have become great friends and, above anything, these friendships are what I value most from my time spent in his employment. To think I questioned whether I was in the right place when I was starting out was, looking back, probably down to the fear of the unknown. But having taken the leap of faith, I am so pleased I did. I went with my gut and I don't regret it.

what are you trying to portray as a photographer?

I WOULD like to think that, when someone looks at an image I have taken, they feel inspired and that a certain positive light radiates from it. Whether it be through a headshot of a model, a portrait of the head of a fashion brand or a still life shot of some face cream. If it doesn't stir some sort of feeling, then I have not succeeded in my job as an image creator.

images: Katrina Lawson Johnston

does having a Christian faith make any difference?

WITHOUT my faith, my life would be one big worry pot. It makes all the difference to me to know that I am loved as I am, and that I have a Saviour who has given his life so that I can have a relationship with God.

do your beliefs and work sometimes clash?

NOT really, as I always think and pray about which jobs to take on. It is important to listen to that little voice of calm when choosing work and clients. On the few occasions that I haven't, I have learnt my lesson.

SETTING OUT ON MY OWN

AFTER five great years with Jacob, and growing responsibility, I decided it was time to go it alone as a photographer. It seemed illogical on paper, but I knew in my heart that the time was right. It was a huge step for me, pulling myself away from the comfort of the studio manager/assistant role, especially as travel was becoming increasingly frequent (and trips were always fun). I had recently got married and this also added to the decision.

ALTHOUGH IT WOULD HAVE BEEN FUN I KNOW, IN HINDSIGHT, THAT I LEFT AT THE RIGHT TIME

Shortly after I left, Jacob started to go off to Los Angeles for long periods. And I would have been going with him. Although it would have been fun I know, in hindsight, that I left at the right time. I was blessed to find a fantastic guy to take over from me in the role, and I know that he has been amazing.

The trickiest thing when starting out (without an agent) is finding work, but I was fortunate that a number of friends had started up British-based fashion brands that I began to work with. I love branding, understanding who the brand are trying to reach, and what needs to happen in order for them to succeed. But when all that comes together on shoot day with the model, hair, make-up, styling and photo team, I remember what it is that really makes it the best job, and that is the people and the collaborative way we can work towards getting the best out of each other.

AS FOR THE FUTURE, WHO KNOWS WHERE I WILL END UP!

I have a particular friend who started a scented candle range and, when we shoot together, we can be brutally honest, especially if something is not working. Yet, this only fuels us to make sure we get it right. It is always exciting to see what we end up with at the end of a day in the studio together.

As for the future, who knows where I will end up! I will aim to keep widening my network, shooting for model agencies and working with other creative friends who inspire me. I have many hopes and dreams, but I don't want to be limited by what I plan for myself. There may be another way that I don't yet know or understand and that is also a really exciting thought.

LOVE THE LORD YOUR GOD
WITH ALL YOUR PASSION AND
PRAYER AND INTELLIGENCE
LOVE OTHERS AS WELL
AS YOU LOVE YOURSELF

image: Katrina Lawson Johnston

God's top commandment for fashion?

I believe we are simply called to love one another.

Matthew 22: 37-40 (The Message)
Jesus said, "'Love the Lord your God with
all your passion and prayer and intelligence.'
This is the most important, the first on any
list. But there is a second to set alongside it:
'Love others as well as you love yourself.'
These two commands are pegs; everything in
God's Law and the Prophets hangs from them."

A bible verse that has empowered my journey

Do not despise these small beginnings,
for the Lord rejoices to see the work begin

Zechariah 4:10 (New Living Translation)

image: Katrina Lawson Johnston

I HAVE MANY HOPES AND DREAMS,
BUT I DON'T WANT TO BE LIMITED
BY WHAT I PLAN FOR MYSELF.
THERE MAY BE ANOTHER WAY
THAT I DON'T YET KNOW OR
UNDERSTAND AND THAT IS ALSO
A REALLY EXCITING THOUGHT

katrina lawson johnston

A PRAYER FOR PHOTOGRAPHERS

FATHER GOD
Please guide me to always be
kind and loving in everything I do.

To always see the beauty in
something, to inspire and to be
inspired, to be open and humble.

May you bless all those who see the
world through a lens, may you give
them an abundance of creativity
and may we all encourage each other
to work with integrity and honesty.

Amen

FINLAY & CO

Finlay & Co is a London-based brand designing, manufacturing and distributing iconic sunglasses.

The company was set up by four friends: Tom Stannard, Dave Lochhead, Sam Lawson Johnston & Dane Butler.

interview with Dane Butler

THE STRENGTH
OF THE FOUR HAS
BEEN THE MOST
AMAZING PART
OF OUR JOURNEY

image: fashionweekdaily.com   *Sam, Dane, Tom & Dave*

HOW FOUR FRIENDS FOUND THEMSELVES IN FASHION

THE four founders, who became friends through London church, Holy Trinity Brompton, come from a diverse range of backgrounds, including marketing within the consumer technology industry, retail banking, property and the charity sector.

With the exception of Sam, who had previously set up a tailoring business on Savile Row, but predominantly works in commercial property, none of the founders had any previous experience within the fashion industry.

The idea came about when Dave and Dane were on holiday in Portugal. Dave was on gardening leave from Barclays and Dane was disappointed he wasn't being paid to go on holiday!

Both had a history of entrepreneurial endeavours and were actively looking to start a new business.

They started to throw around ideas while sitting round the pool, enjoying a few drinks, and quickly their thoughts turned to eyewear. It struck them that most of their friends were creative and expressive with their clothes; yet they all just wore a classic pair of Wayfarer sunglasses. There was no individuality or expression.

Quickly realising that there wasn't a British brand that would naturally be the go-to eyewear brand for their friends, they began planning the launch of Finlay & Co.

A DISRUPTIVE ENTRY PRODUCT

Dane takes up the story ...

SHORTLY after our return to the UK, we headed to our church's annual week away, HTB Focus, and the four of us began to work on the idea from there.

A disruptive initial offering was key, and that came when Dave returned from the US with a pair of wooden sunglasses. We loved the concept of using wood. However, we knew that the brand needed to be tailored to a 20-30 year old London influencer, rather than the skater vibe brands that we were seeing in the States.

We began sampling materials and soon knew that we were onto something. During the initial stages, we would regularly meet as a four in cafés, and the staff and fellow café dwellers alike would gravitate towards the sunglasses, picking them up and playing with them, they couldn't believe it was made from real wood!

THE YOUNG QUARTET THAT MAKE THE SUNGLASSES ARE VERY TALENTED
Anna Wintour

Right from the outset we tried to hold the business idea lightly and enjoy the journey; celebrating every little success and praying before meetings, not your typical business model that you read in many start-up books!

We decided to be really open and honest about our lack of industry experience, rather than trying to gloss over it. There was a part of us that wondered how we would be received. A key example of this was when we were fortunate enough to meet Anna Wintour, American Vogue Editor, when we were invited by Vogue Talents Corner in Milan, as one of ten upcoming brands. She had worked her way around the other nine designers in the room, who had all trained at the best fashion design schools around the world, and we were feeling just a little intimidated. When she asked where I studied, I replied "Oxford Brookes". She really enjoyed hearing our unconventional story!

'FINLAY' MEANS *RAY OF SUNLIGHT* IN GAELIC

EARLY CHALLENGES

IN the early days, we all had other jobs, so had to squeeze our planning into evenings and weekends. As you can imagine, this was pretty full-on, especially for our girlfriends/wives, but thankfully they were all very patient and supportive!

One of our hardest initial challenges was thinking up the right name. It's one thing coming up with a name you like, it's another finding a name you like that has the web domain available, no existing IP etc. After many months spent exploring different options, we fell in love with the name Finlay & Co.

'Finlay' means *ray of sunlight* in Gaelic, which was perfect.

Then there was the challenge of finding somewhere to produce our sunglasses. Despite some strong early Balsa wood prototyping from Sam, we knew that finding the right people to make the sunglasses was going to be key.

We had a dilemma - should we go to a factory producing wooden products and try to teach them about eyewear, or, go to an eyewear factory and try to teach them about wood?

In the end we opted for the latter, and the Lord led us through a terrifying number of stands at our first eyewear industry show to find our first production facility.

image: Katrina Lawson Johnston

125

FIRST SUCCESSES?

I remember the day our first ever web sale came through. It was a euphoric moment. We have an app on our phones which tracks all sales coming through the website, and checking it is one of the most addictive things in the world!

I think we all go through stages of having to go cold turkey and ban ourselves from looking at it, especially when you're with mates, it's fairly boring chat!

Taking on our first stockist, Orlebar Brown, was pretty incredible too. It's a brand we admire, founded by Adam Brown, who has a not dissimilar story to us. He was on holiday, looking across the pool and on noticing the lack of well-designed beach shorts, decided to launch a brand to fill that gap in the market. He was very generous with his advice, and it was such a fantastic store to be in.

Jesus pointed to a simple lifestyle, how does that sit alongside Luxury Fashion?

I should probably consult a theologian!

We try and sit as an accessible luxury brand. I don't think there is anything wrong with having nice possessions.

If they become more important in your life than God, then I think it's an issue, but that is true of many different areas in life; physical fitness, your job, your children, etc.

They are all in themselves great things, but if any become THE thing and elevated above God, then it's not great.

God's top commandment for fashion?

IT'S a classic, but I think the most important commandment is to 'love your neighbour as yourself'. Whether they are a colleague or a competitor, someone from the same background or someone from a different background, someone from the same belief system or someone with a different/no belief system. We should 'put on love' (*Colossians 3:12-14*) and let people come as they are.

I also like the chat in Hebrews 12:1. Run the race marked out for you. Run your race not someone else's. Cheer them on in theirs, but don't try and run their race. You have your own to run, a race that's unique for you. If we try and run someone else's race, or compare ourselves to them, then it robs us of what we are called to do on this earth, and robs the world of what we were meant to be.

a Bible verse that has empowered your journey?

Whatever you do, work at it with all your heart, as working for the Lord Colossians 3:23

That's a good one to keep you going when it's 11pm on a Monday night!

author's suggestion!

The sun stopped in the middle of the sky and delayed going down a full day Joshua 10:13

perfect conditions for FINLAY & Co.

GROWING MOMENTUM

WE have been very fortunate, in that it feels like we have had really strong momentum the whole way through the journey so far. There are times when it has felt like plain sailing, and others when it's been a tough slog. Especially in the early days when none of us were working on Finlay & Co. full time. It could feel like pushing water up hill!

However, we had a few early breaks, such as David Gandy wearing our sunglasses to London Collections Men. Having the world's top male model wearing your frames and all the fashion magazines ringing you up to find out more about your collection really opened a lot of doors!

In fact, it led to us being selected for Grazia's fashion charts in the third week of our existence. We were so excited (once we had checked out what the Grazia fashion charts actually were).

It was so early on that we didn't actually have a website up and running. I remember being told it must be live before they went to print, then having to spend a few very late nights with my brother-in-law, who built our first site for us, desperately trying to finish it in time. It was right down to the wire, but we made it, just!

Showing at London Fashion Week was a great privilege and opened the door to shows in Milan, Paris and New York. From there, momentum really grew with some key stockists; from Harvey Nichols and Wolf and Badger in the UK, to Barneys in the US.

We now find ourselves stocked in over 130 stores in over twenty different countries.

*a number of Christians
are starting up fashion
businesses - what's going on?*

Good question. God is a creative being
and we are made in his likeness. So, to
be creative is to be fully human, made
in the image of God.

Historically, there have been many
incredible businesses founded by people
of faith; Barclays, Lloyds, Cadbury,
Rowntree, Richer Sounds, Stagecoach.

However, it feels like in recent years most
of the creativity within and coming out of
the church has been in the area of music ...
certainly, that which you hear about, anyway.

It feels like over the last three to five years
there has been a shift though, and now we are
seeing a move towards more entrepreneurial
activities. I guess it goes hand in hand with
what we are seeing outside the church too,
a landscape where young people no longer
want to work for the same employer for
forty years and then collect a good pension.
They want flexibility, freedom to be their
own boss, to be creative, take risks, and
work in a fun environment. Advances
in technology have made the barriers to
entry much lower for most sectors too
which helps create an environment,
where entrepreneurship can flourish.

Large swathes of the Bible are about not
being afraid, taking risks, not worrying
about the future, holding things lightly and
trusting in God etc. All things that I think
are helpful to an entrepreneur as otherwise
it can become all-consuming and scary!

image: Katrina Lawson Johnston

IF WE TRY AND RUN SOMEONE
ELSE'S RACE, OR COMPARE
OURSELVES TO THEM, THEN
IT ROBS US OF WHAT WE ARE
CALLED TO DO ON THIS EARTH,
AND ROBS THE WORLD OF WHAT
WE WERE MEANT TO BE

dane butler finlay & co

A PRAYER FOR
FASHION BUSINESSES
WITH A MISSION

FATHER GOD

Thank you for ordaining that creativity
should act as a bridge between Yourself
and the practicalities of everyday life ...
and that businesses can be a vehicle of
blessing for those who would do things
to the benefit of all.

Grant bigness of vision, clarity of purpose
and determination to carry on despite
the challenges, to all those who would
set aside personal gain and status to give,
through their businesses, opportunity to
all those they work with, and excellent,
fairly produced and sustainably sourced
products to their customers.

All are made in the image of God, yet
each of us is different. Give us courage to
develop our own uniqueness, and guard
us from the temptation to look at what
others are doing and, by seeking to imitate
them, shrinking the glorious breadth of
variety and richness You have given us
the potential to share. Amen

FASHION
FOR
CHRIST

CHRISSIE ABBOTT

Founder of FASHION FOR CHRIST, Chrissie has twenty-five years experience working for international fashion and luxury brands, winning the loyalty of VIPs worldwide (including royalty, celebrities and high profile business executives). Chrissie has worked across Retail, Management, Couture, PR, Buying, Marketing, Wholesale and Styling, was a well known Personal Shopper and has appeared on TV, radio interviews and in many magazines and newspapers. In 2007, Chrissie decided it was time to help support Christians working in fashion. We find out why and how she set about it.

I PRAYED LONG AND HARD FOR GOD TO BRING CHRISTIANS OUT OF THE SHADOWS AND INTO THE LIGHT. THE MORE I PRAYED, THE MORE CAME OUT. I AM ASTONISHED AT HOW MANY CHRISTIANS THERE ARE IN FASHION

HOW DID THE IDEA OF A FASHION SUPPORT NETWORK COME ABOUT?

AFTER speaking at a Faith & Work breakfast for the Sport, Media and Fashion industries at my home church, Holy Trinity Brompton, HTB's Director of Prayer, Pete Greig told me he was surprised at the number of people at the event working in fashion. He asked if I'd consider getting something together, and the HTB Fashion Network was born. The next year we had our first breakfast specifically for fashion, with Simon Ward, COO of the British Fashion Council as the keynote speaker. The average attendance at these events was sixty. 150 turned out. I was thrilled ... Pete was astonished.

As was HTB vicar, Nicky Gumbel when, soon after, he found himself reporting that the best attended prayer breakfasts had been politics, law, banking, medicine and ... (is this correct?) fashion! God's sense of humour surfaced again when Nicky was interviewing me during a talk and asked what I thought of his dress sense. "Well, that would be a completely different sermon!"

A GREAT START - WHAT CAME NEXT?

IN 2010, we formed a small committee and decided to push the boat out, and hold a prayer meeting during London Fashion Week. We were thrilled when Somerset House agreed to allow us to use a room on site during the event and laughed when the room allocated was the Salt Room (salt and light at the heart of LFW!)

As I walked across the famous Somerset House courtyard the week before to spy out the room, thinking to myself "can we do this?" God said to me quite clearly; "what's taken you so long?"!

It was a well attended, powerful time of sharing and prayer, and we have continued each season since.

I GOT CAUGHT UP IN THE GLITZ AND GLAM OF THE FASHION INDUSTRY WHEN I WAS EIGHTEEN. IT DREW ME AWAY FROM MY FAITH

YOUR TRUTH NEVER GOES OUT OF FASHION
Psalm 119:90 (The Message)

GOD HAS PUT ME IN THIS INDUSTRY FOR THIRTY YEARS AND HE'S NOT CALLED ME OUT YET. I BELIEVE HE HAS CALLED ME TO BE A LIGHT IN THE INDUSTRY

YOU MUST HAVE EXPERIENCED GROWTH PAINS?

I WAS astonished at the interest in the group with some 400 members joining the Facebook network. Indeed, there were so many people wanting to be part of it, I spent most of my spare time checking out if the applicants had a meaningful link to fashion. A lot seemed to be hangers on, and I was concerned that the members of the group might be exploited. But God challenged me, asking why I was putting up these restrictions. "Why are you closing the door?" He led me to realise, not too dissimilar to Peter on the rooftop at Joppa *(Acts 10)*, that He was using the accessibility and attractiveness of fashion to reach out to those on the edges.

As the group grew, it seemed right to sever the formal link to HTB and for a while I grappled with what it should be a called. Then, suddenly, it came to me - *FASHION FOR CHRIST* - obvious!

By the time we changed the name, there were 800 people linked to the group.

THOSE WEREN'T THE ONLY PAINS?

UNFORTUNATELY, not. Coinciding with the launch of the HTB Fashion Network, I started to get debilitating migraines. In spite of numerous visits to doctors, chiropractors, and being endlessly prayed over, these persisted until I felt the clear call to hand on the baton of day to day leadership of the group.

I calculated that I had suffered migraines for no less than 380 days over a seven year period. Like the apostle Paul, *(2 Corinthians 12)*, I had to learn that Jesus' grace was sufficient for me, and his power was made perfect in my weakness.

It's been a roller-coaster, laughing out loud at God's sense of humour one week; then confined to a darkened room the next.

FASHION FOR CHRIST

- *A PLACE WHERE CHRISTIANS IN FASHION CAN FIND, CONNECT WITH AND PRAY FOR LIKE MINDED PEOPLE*

- *A PLACE OF ENCOURAGEMENT AND INSPIRATION*

- *A SAFE PLACE TO SHARE CHALLENGES AND NEEDS*

- *A NETWORK OF CHRISTIANS WHO CAN GUIDE AND COUNSEL YOUNGER CHRISTIANS STUDYING OR STARTING OUT IN THE FASHION WORLD*

- *BE THE DIFFERENCE AND PUT FASHION ON THE MAP AS AN INDUSTRY WHERE GOD IS AT THE CORE AND DOING GREAT THINGS*

- *SURPRISE AND DELIGHT PEOPLE THAT GOD CARES GREATLY ABOUT FASHION*

- *REGAIN GOD'S GROUND IN AN INDUSTRY THAT HAS SPIRITUALLY BEEN LACKING AND SEE TRANSFORMATION AND HIS GLORY*

- *BE EVANGELISTS TO THE FASHION INDUSTRY*

I AM PASSIONATE
ABOUT LEVERAGING
MY PERSONAL SKILLS
AND EXPERIENCE TO
HELP OTHERS, IN
PARTICULAR TO
MENTOR YOUNG
PEOPLE AND HELP
THEM REACH THEIR
FULL POTENTIAL
IN LIFE

images: fashion for christ

HIGH HEELS AND BISHOPS?

AH YES! As part of the Diocese of London's 2020 Vision initiative to reach out to the creative industries, I was invited to speak to the London Synod, complete with bishops. Whilst I felt a little intimidated, I decided to go for it, wore my highest heels, dressed in fur from head to foot, and made a grand entrance. I'd love to have heard the conversations in the corridor afterwards!

Seriously, though, I think many in the church discount those working in fashion, mainly as they don't understand the industry and there seem to be so many challenges for a Christian. But that is exactly why I believe God is powerfully at work in fashion and is using it as a trailblazer to show how Christians throughout the creative industries, and indeed more widely, can bring their faith alive in their work.

HOW IS FASHION FOR CHRIST FARING TODAY?

EARLY on, I had linked up with the leadership of Models for Christ, which is based out of the USA. In 2010, MfC's international directors, Christina and Shane Nearman moved to England, so Christina could pursue a master's degree in Nottingham.

When I felt the time had come to stand down from day to day leadership, they took over and have used their experience in America to establish monthly gatherings, where about thirty members meet up for fellowship, listening to a testimony, share and pray. These are powerful times, building on the seasonal prayer meetings at London Fashion Week.

gMODA

SHANE & CHRISTINA NEARMAN

Shane and Christina Nearman are the International Directors of gMODA (formerly Models for Christ). Both have modelled successfully around the world for over half their lives. They have sacrificed the 'American Dream' to support and encourage people through the opportunities and challenges within the fashion and entertainment industry. This includes providing support to those struggling with difficult issues, such as eating disorders, suicide attempts, and addictions, and sharing the hope of the Gospel.

WWW. GMODA.ORG

BUT HOW CAN THEY CALL ON HIM TO
SAVE THEM UNLESS THEY BELIEVE IN HIM?
AND HOW CAN THEY BELIEVE IN HIM IF
THEY HAVE NEVER HEARD ABOUT HIM?
AND HOW CAN THEY HEAR ABOUT HIM
UNLESS SOMEONE TELLS THEM?
Romans 10:14

gMODA (formerly Models for Christ) is a global community of professionals who seek to honour God as they navigate the unique opportunities and challenges within the fashion related industry. Founded in 1984, gMODA has provided support, encouragement and community to fashion professionals around the world, through outreach and discipleship, to reflect the light and love of Jesus Christ within popular culture.

WE KNOW THAT THE FASHION INDUSTRY, AND THE PEOPLE WHO MAKE THEIR LIVING IN IT, ARE RARELY RECOGNISED AS BEING 'IN NEED'

gMODA groups gather to host projects of compassionate service, industry relevant Bible studies, outreach dinner events, and facilitate leadership and discipleship training. gMODA communities provide members with a strong network of support and encouragement as they travel.

THE CHURCH has mobilised people and resources to reach out to people and places in need. It is a noble mission, and an important one, but we know that the fashion industry, and the people who make their living in it, are rarely recognised as being 'in need'.

Through our experience as professionals in the fashion industry - models, photographers, hair and makeup artists, designers, stylists, agents and industry representatives - we know this could not be less true.

gMODA is a bridge to the un-churched who would not attend a church service but, after investing into their lives, become part of a church community. Lives are changed.

The ultimate goal of all our work is to go out and follow the mandate of Jesus Christ to spread His Gospel and make disciples of the nations.

All of our programmes serve this goal in some way, chiefly by preparing and equipping our members to shine the light of Christ wherever they travel, or by physically going out into the community or workplace in the spirit of 'reflecting Christ in fashion'.

PREPARING AND EQUIPPING OUR MEMBERS TO SHINE THE LIGHT OF CHRIST WHEREVER THEY TRAVEL

gMODA (MODELS FOR CHRIST) TIMELINE
DEVELOPMENT OF A GLOBAL SUPPORT NETWORK

1984 **First Models For Christ (gMODA) meeting in NYC**

1986 MFC meetings grow to 100+; NYC community service outreaches begin

1987 MFC obtains 501-C3 non-profit incorporated status

1999 Atlanta chapter starts; focus on reaching fashion professionals globally

2002 NYC chapter adopts seeker-friendly name, 'Paradox'

2003 Los Angeles chapter starts; outreach dinners and community service projects begin; fashion professionals from U.S. cities take mission trip to Mexico; Dallas chapter starts

2005 Miami chapter starts; MFC focuses on international development in Paris with outreach team

2006 MFC develops new Board, branding, and website

2007 International media glimpses MFC vision giving heightened press coverage

2008 MFC produces first NYC Fashion Week outreach

2009 25th Anniversary celebration in NYC

2010 First MFC NYC Fashion Night of Prayer; MFC NYC restructured into intimate small groups; Paradox name is ended in favour of MFC NYC; first intern hired

2011 NYC, LA, Miami host Fashion Night of Prayer before Fashion Week; American Bible Society/MFC partner for MFC Fashion Week outreach; MFC LA begins Fashion Week outreaches

2012 Nearmans move to UK to launch greater Global MFC Vision; London partnership with Fashion For Christ develops. Partners with FFC to start prayer at London Fashion Week

2013 Chapters launched in Paris, Milano (gMODA), Sydney, Brazil, Chicago, Dallas, Hawaii

2014 MFC 30th Anniversary; Sydney Fashion Night of Prayer and Fashion Week outreaches begin; Milano starts Fashion Night of Prayer

2015 Start Faith In Fashion series in London with FFC; Hawaii Fashion Night of Prayer begins

2016 NYC, LA, Miami, Hawaii, Milano, Sydney Fashion Nights of Prayer NYC, LA and Sydney Fashion Week outreaches; MFC NY, LA, Miami, Chicago, Dallas, Hawaii, Brazil, Paris, Milano & FFC London continue growth. **Models for Christ rebrands internationally with the name gMODA**

"I have developed friends at MFC, who I serve alongside and who are so positive for my life - people who love me, walk with me, and hold me accountable and surround me." Lucas

BETTINA MARAYAG, a former fashion buyer for one of the largest retail companies in New York City, came to know Jesus, and went on to travel the world as Pastor David Wilkerson's International conference and missions director. Through the ministry of World Challenge, Bettina helped to facilitate unity within the churches in cities around the globe, to bring the Gospel and revival to all nations. She was also responsible for overseeing 126 feeding sites in 26 nations, feeding 20,000 children and refugees. She travelled extensively to facilitate help and aid to refugees in the Middle East and other war torn lands.

A LIFE TRANSFORMED

I spent almost a decade working as a buyer in New York City. While it was exciting - buying and selling, travel, fashion shows ... and all the perks that came with it - it still left me wanting. There was an emptiness inside that could not seem to be filled. I went through the motions, making the most of it, but I had an intense feeling that there had to be more to life.

A friend introduced me to a girl he was dating, a fashion designer, who shared about Jesus, and the need to be born again. I did not want the "born again" stuff, having heard about a large Christian television evangelist, who had recently been arrested for fraud.

The next day, I was invited to a Bible study with Models for Christ (now gMODA). I looked around all these beautiful people, singing, praying, reading the Bible. They looked happy and peaceful, and there was such a sweet presence that felt really good.

A fashion photographer invited me to come with him, the next day, to a small church, which met at a music studio. Many there were actors and musicians on Broadway. I was so blown away ... and scared at the same time.

That day I had an encounter with God, and I knew that something supernatural happened. I was surrounded by new people who loved God, and became a part of the core group of Models for Christ. We often met for fellowship but, most of all, Jeff and Laura Calenberg (MFC's Founders) opened their home, shared the Word of God, and prayed.

It was through MFC that I got grounded in God's Word, as prayer, reaching out to others, and sharing the Gospel are key components of the ministry. We were not just hearers of the Word, but do-ers of the Word. My life changed, my heart is filled, my mind transformed, and I live each day with purpose.

I know I can do all things through Christ, who gives me strength. *(Philippians 4:13)* He gives me grace and courage during tough times and challenges. Above all, the comfort of knowing that it is well with my soul, and I shall be with Him one day. MFC/gMODA was my foundation, and I carry on, to this day, the impact of this ministry.

SERVING THOSE IN NEED

FOR over three decades, gMODA NYC (known as Models for Christ) has supported and served the Bowery Mission, a non-profit organisation established in 1879, which faithfully ministers to men, women and children caught in cycles of poverty, hopelessness and dependencies in all five boroughs of New York City.

Our gMODA community service has included: providing models, makeup, stylists, hair, etc. for fashion show fundraisers; food preparation for meal distribution during their annual Thanksgiving week outreach, which provides 10,000 meals; starting our annual 'Gloves and Socks Drive' and 'Toiletry Drive' within gMODA to meet practical needs of the homeless; handing out the Bowery's location card to the homeless with shelter and clinic information during winter months; and serving evening meals in-house to 120+ homeless men, women and children each quarter.

Whether we are praying with the homeless after serving meals, providing toiletries and clothing, or rolling up our sleeves to tear meat off bones for meal prep, we count it a joy and privilege to serve the Kingdom of God alongside our many global partners, including the Bowery Mission (*www.bowery.org*) in New York City!

WHETHER WE ARE PRAYING WITH THE HOMELESS ... OR ROLLING UP OUR SLEEVES TO TEAR MEAT OFF BONES FOR MEAL PREP WE COUNT IT A JOY AND PRIVILEGE TO SERVE

THIS FASHION BUSINESS -
IT'S A MATTER OF
LIFE & DEATH
Lucy Siegle

BIG ISSUES

image: fashionrevolution.org

5

TEN OF FASHION'S BIG ISSUES

challenges faced by a global industry
... and its consumers

image: fashionrevolution.org

ON April 24th 2013, 1,134 people were killed and hundreds were injured when the Rana Plaza garment manufacturing building in Savar, Bangladesh collapsed. It is considered the deadliest ever garment factory accident, as well as the most lethal accidental structural failure in modern human history.

The building contained clothing factories, a bank, apartments, and several other shops. The shops and the bank on the lower floors closed immediately after cracks were discovered in the building. Garment workers were ordered to return the following day and the building collapsed during the morning rush hour.

HOW DID YOU FIRST BECOME INTERESTED IN WRITING ABOUT THE EFFECTS OF THE FASHION INDUSTRY?

AS a young journalist I began writing about green living and ethical consumerism. I became a sort of agony aunt for the environment. Having worked my way through the nation's store cupboards, turning things Fairtrade and organic, I finally got to sorting out the average closet. The stories I unravelled about the fashion supply chain were unbelievable, in terms of egregious pollution and blind exploitation, and the story has just got bigger and bigger. Follow the money, follow the oil, follow the fashion.

LUCY SIEGLE

LUCY, a London-based author, journalist and presenter, has written a weekly ethical living column for the Observer for over a decade, and authored two books. A Humanist, Lucy was an Executive Producer on *The True Cost*, a feature length documentary film exploring the impact of fashion on people and the planet, including the Rana Plaza disaster.

this edited interview is reproduced from
http://truecostmovie.com/lucy-siegle-interview

I was struck by how quickly a sustainable system can be undone and destroyed forever. Local textile and garment cultures are pretty much annihilated by the just-in-time, outsourced model of today's global brands and retailers - the companies that pretend they are in the business of creating opportunities in low-wage economies.

I realised most western buyers were using completely nonsensical calculations when they placed orders in first tier factories. This means the factory they look around can't possibly complete the gigantic orders they place, and will obviously out-source. This is a classic point at which sweatshop labour becomes a reality. I realised there were a number of flashpoints in the supply chain that were adding up to extreme exploitation and possible catastrophe, and that this was a standard business model.

SINCE RANA PLAZA HAS THERE BEEN SUBSTANTIAL CHANGE?

NO. Opportunities were missed to re-invent the supply chain and I cannot say with any confidence that there will not be a repeat of Rana Plaza in terms of scale. Hundreds of people have lost their lives, been injured or had their health compromised by producing garments since Rana Plaza, and the garment industry remains dangerous, polluting and energy intensive, when it need not be any of these.

I feel now that there should have been a greater push to make brands and retailers accountable legally, rather than allowing yet more voluntary codes of conduct.

'SUSTAINABLE FASHION' - A CONTRADICTION OR A REAL POSSIBILITY?

THE GARMENT INDUSTRY REMAINS DANGEROUS, POLLUTING AND ENERGY INTENSIVE WHEN IT NEED NOT BE ANY OF THESE

IT is a real possibility because:

a) sewing clothes is not inherently dangerous, so I believe we can stop killing people in the supply chain if we want to;

b) other industries with much more complex supply chains have come up with very clever ways of lowering impact and pollution;

c) if we empower designers, they are incredibly innovative, problem solving people, and will natural gravitate toward sustainability.

But the following needs to stop: fashion has been co-opted by turbo charged capitalist corporations who are kicking the shit out of it and stripping fashion of its culture. This will be the end of all fashion, sustainable or otherwise.

A LOT OF BRANDS ARE SPEAKING MORE OPENLY ABOUT THEIR CSR EFFORTS. IS THIS REAL DEDICATION TO CHANGE OR SIMPLY MORE SOPHISTICATED PR?

THERE are a few essential truths here:

a) it's easy for brands/retailers to look at 'green' issues, including using novel eco fibres and recycling waste clothes, before living wages and the tricky people stuff;

b) when they are looking at wages in a few pilot schemes, but pushing on into new low-wage fashion production hubs, such as Myanmar and Ethiopia, we have to spot the contradiction;

c) if your business model is based on furious expansion, really how will that ever square with being sustainable?

With some notable exceptions, the fashion media remains rather silo-ed, focused on aesthetics, shows, celebrities – all that jazz. Increasingly, its job is to flog product, so it tends to be uncritical.

Meanwhile, the big names in apparel retail are part of huge groups, possibly involved in other sectors with huge, corporate influence, lobbyists and all that attends global players.

Both luxury and fast fashion have become investor driven in the last four to five years, and this is the market they tend to respond to. I'd argue many of these corporations aren't really interested in fashion, just shifting money about, which leads us into politics.

ETHICAL CHALLENGES

LUCY SIEGLE'S TOP 10

CHALLENGES
FOR BRANDS
RETAILERS &
CONSUMERS
... WE CAN
ALL MAKE A
DIFFERENCE

THINKING CONSUMERISM

I have £20 in my pocket. How might I spend it? Three choices:

- I can run with the herd and buy yet another item of unneeded clothing that swells the coffers of a multinational company who have huge vested interest in perpetuating ever growing spend.
- I can choose to empower someone else by continuing with a purchase, but buy a fairtrade product that guarantees a better deal to producers.
- I can purchase a Green Bond, created to fund projects that have positive environmental and/or climate benefits.

THIRTY WEARS RULE

DON'T buy anything you can't commit to wearing at least thirty times - that way you are respecting the hands that have made the product and the enviromental impact to the planet.

A LIVING WAGE FOR ALL

EVERY brand should aspire to best practice, rather than what they can get away with - not least of which should be by paying a living wage to all those involved throughout a product's supply chain.

WITH POWER COMES RESPONSIBILITY

RETAILERS and brands need to acknowledge the power they have in host countries and apply it responsibly.

COLLABORATION NOT DISTRUST

IT'S time to move on from being defensive and protective and try collaborations even, maybe especially, with those who have not been trusted previously. It happens elsewhere: Greenpeace now collaborate with local fishermen; green energy industrialist Dale Vince, and his company Ecotricity, now work closely with the RSPB on the development of wind farms to minimise impact on local bird populations.

IF WE PRODUCE CLOTHES THAT LOOK LIKE LITTER
THEY WILL BE TREATED LIKE TRASH

ACKNOWLEDGE THE SUPPLY CHAIN
FROM the cotton farmer to the consumer, everyone
involved in a garment's production and distribution should
be recognised and acknowledged - not just the designer.

MORE THAN THE CATWALK
THERE is currently only one mechanism for celebrating all the
creativity and endeavour that makes up the world of fashion
- the catwalk. The twice-yearly catwalk shows only add fuel to
the fire of fast fashion and resultant disposability and waste.
How might we celebrate the whole of a garment's lifetime?

PLANNED OBSOLESCENCE
HOW can we take the pressure off the system? There is no great
data, but we know that we are consuming clothes faster and
they are lasting less time than at any previous point in history.
And it is not just the big high street retailers. Increasingly, when
a designer joins a big brand, they come under pressure to create
more and more, not better and better. Who will stand up and
challenge this unsustainable, headlong rush?

TREATED LIKE TRASH
CONSIDER ... if we produce clothes that look like litter,
they will be treated like trash.

WHO OWNS FASHION?
IS it creatives, craftspeople and those with a love of fashion?
Or shady investment groups with a vested interest in a
quick return from the biggest, fastest turn round of stock?

12

IS FASHION DESTROYING
THE ENVIRONMENT?

IN PURSUIT OF SUSTAINABLE FASHION

10,000 GARMENTS GO TO LANDFILL EVERY FIVE MINUTES

PRODUCTION HAS BEEN CENTRAL FOR YOU FROM DAY ONE?

SINCE I started in 1997, I have been fixated on how I produce my collections. Although, initially, it centred on what it meant to me poetically, rather than environmentally, I always wanted to use pre-existing materials. This was breaking the rules at the time, and the longer I went on, the more I felt this intense urge grow.

With From Somewhere, we have only ever used pre-consumer waste, always produced locally, and in a very socially minded way. When we started out, our production was in Italy, helping to rehabilitate disadvantaged individuals through a local cooperative.

ORSOLA DE CASTRO

ORSOLA is founder of From Somewhere, a designer brand making clothes from recycled offcuts of luxury materials. With her partner, Filippo Ricci, she curates Estethica, an initiative set up in association with the British Fashion Council to showcase eco-fashion brands. With Carry Somers, she co-founded Fashion Revolution Day, which aims to celebrate best practice, highlight the most pressing issues and campaign for change within the fashion industry.

YOU FOUNDED ESTETHICA IN LONDON - A PLATFORM FOR DESIGNERS WITH ETHICAL AND SUSTAINABLE STANDARDS

ESTETHICA started in 2006, the first ever curated eco fashion area, right at the heart of London Fashion Week. It launched designers such as Christopher Raeburn, and we have supported over 100 brands since its inception. It has taken time for sustainable principles to become a founding force in the design mentality - we had to be patient.

CONSUMERS ARE KEY?

ABSOLUTELY. Before we buy, all of us need to ask ourselves: "Who made this garment? How was it made? Was there dignity in their toil?"

Clothes are our chosen skin. No one should be content to wear someone else's misery.

TARGETS FOR THE NEXT FIVE YEARS?

GOVERNMENTS must start seriously to address the injustice in global supply chains - financial equality - just as they have done with gender equality.

... AND IN TEN YEARS?

THE industry will have started to slow down, leaving space for individuality, artisanal skills ... and greater sanity for industry and consumer alike.

HOW WILL CHANGE COME ABOUT?

A ripple effect: consumers raise awareness - this puts pressure on brands to act - they will need to engage with institutions and governments to ensure an even playing field to support stable change.

WHAT IF NOTHING CHANGES?

WE will not just hasten the ruination of our planet, we will be regressing as a species. It would be nothing less than a failure of humanity.

CLOTHES ARE OUR
CHOSEN SKIN
NO ONE SHOULD
BE CONTENT TO
WEAR SOMEONE
ELSE'S MISERY

BUY CLOTHES WITH
LONGING AND DESIRE,
DON'T BUY ON A WHIM ...
ALWAYS BUY THINKING
YOU WILL PASS IT ON
TO SOMEONE ELSE

A FAVOURITE QUOTE?

IN NATURE, NOTHING IS
CREATED AND NOTHING
IS DESTROYED ...
BUT EVERYTHING
IS TRANSFORMED
Antoine De Lavoisier

T-SHIRT POWER

FASHION'S LOUD HAILER

EVER since Katharine Hamnett marched into a London Fashion Week reception at 10 Downing Street in 1984, confronting Margaret Thatcher with an over-sized t-shirt bearing an over-sized message - 58% DON'T WANT PERSHING - the slogan t-shirt has been shouting out messages from the profound to the profane, the comical to the cringeworthy.

Is this all a bit of harmless fun, or an illustration of fashion's potential to influence considerably more than whether we look nice or not?
Here are two current day takes:

i61 is a clothing company run by Deborah Paul. Based on Isaiah 61, a well known chapter in the Bible quoted by Jesus and referring to social justice, freedom and hope, i61's most recent slogan is 'LOVE HAS NO BORDERS', reflecting on the refugee crisis gripping Europe, as thousands flee from turmoil in the Middle East and North Africa.

WHAT DOES DEBORAH HOPE TO ACHIEVE WITH HER T-SHIRTS?

"When I started i61 Clothing, it was clear to me that it would be more than a straightforward fashion brand. I initially started the brand to counteract and challenge what I saw on the high street as negative branding, negative imagery, and a negative use of the female (and sometimes male) body.

For me, fashion is a beautifully creative industry and if we use it for good, we have the power to make a huge impact on the world around us.

We started with simple 'positive' statement t-shirts and sweatshirts and while the brand is evolving, I will always see this as a key part of our offer.

I have a real desire to use fashion to make a positive impact on issues that face our world today. We decided, after seeing the photograph of the young refugee boy washed up on a beach, to launch our LOVE HAS NO BORDERS t-shirt.

We are not necessarily trying to make a political or faith based statement with this t-shirt, though I am very well aware that it may be seen as such.

We are simply making this t-shirt to help those who are in need, in this instance, the refugees. We give 100% of our profit from the sale of this t-shirt to aid the refugees in the Middle East.

A t-shirt will never go out of fashion; every single person on the planet owns a t-shirt in some shape or form. If every season, i61 Clothing can offer a t-shirt that causes people to stop and think, that allows people to help navigate change in a hurting world, then I will be a very happy brand owner.

FASHION, IF WE USE IT FOR GOOD, HAS THE POWER TO MAKE A HUGE IMPACT ON THE WORLD AROUND US

FASHION REVOLUTION campaigns to focus attention on the question "Who made my clothes?" In 2015, some mothers involved in Fashion Revolution challenged two UK high street retailers to trace back to source who made their school uniforms. Founder, Carry Somers reveals what happened:

"One retailer was unable to find out who actually made the clothes they were selling, as there was such a complex web of sub-contractors. Tesco, though, were able to trace the full supplier chain, and they decided to go one step further ..." Dani Baker, Corporate Responsibility Manager of F&F Tesco's F&F, explains:

We are committed to ensure that anyone who supplies any products to F&F has the best possible conditions for their workers. We understand that this cannot be done from afar, but by working in direct partnership with all our suppliers, which is why we have people around the world working on the ground. In Bangladesh, we have a team of about sixty people who not only check things like the fire and safety standards of factories, but also make sure that corners are not cut. So that the factories are a good place to be, with staff being paid a decent wage, on time, and wider social/economic issues being addressed – like ensuring that their children can go to school.

OUR POLO SHIRTS ARE MADE IN BANGLADESH ... FOR EVERY PACK BOUGHT, WE DONATE A UNIFORM TO A CHILD THERE

Studies have shown that children in the developing world, who go to school in uniform, perform better in tests and have lower rates of absenteeism ... we are donating 20,000 school uniforms in Bangladesh as part of our Buy One, Give One scheme. When a customer buys an item from the Buy One, Give One range we will donate an entire uniform. So, as our polo shirts are made in Bangladesh, for every pack bought we donate a uniform to a child there.

interview extract reproduced from http://fashionrevolution.org/ whomademyclothes-tesco-talks

CARRY SOMERS

A British fashion designer, social entrepreneur and fashion campaigner, Carry is founder and director of fair trade hat brand, Pachacuti, and co-founder of the global movement, Fashion Revolution

ON MY FIRST RESEARCH TRIP TO ECUADOR I WITNESSED SHOCKING EXPLOITATION

DISCOVERING INJUSTICE

BORN in Devon, my early days revolved around the evangelical house church my parents set up, initially in their home, and then in the local army hall.

As a teenager, I struggled with what I saw around me as a great deal of superficiality and, I guess looking back, it's not difficult to see that I wasn't going to unquestioningly accept things as they were.

I took two years out before University and worked at a drop-in centre in Devon which I had helped to set up. My instinctive sense of justice quickly flourished into social awareness.

I came back to study for a DipHE in French & Media Studies at Westminster College in Oxford, followed by a BA Hons in Languages and European Studies at Southampton University, and then an MA in Native American Studies at the University of Essex.

During this time, on my first research trip to Ecuador, I witnessed shocking exploitation, as I investigated the development of the local textile industry since the colonial period. These were the early days of fair trade coffee, and it was my first encounter with such a concept.

I got a picture of the low levels of literacy and numeracy, and saw that the prices being paid bore no resemblance to the actual cost of the production. It was a rip off, fundamentally and systemically unjust. The situation was brought into clearer focus whilst I was there. A local cooperative had set up a shop to sell dyes direct to producers, but this posed a threat to the middlemen, who wanted control of the whole supply chain, so they set it on fire.

image: fashionrevolution.org

THE PRICES BEING PAID BORE NO RESEMBLANCE TO THE ACTUAL COST OF THE PRODUCTION. IT WAS A RIP OFF, FUNDAMENTALLY AND SYSTEMICALLY UNJUST

STARTING PACHACUTI

THE research trip to Ecuador was pivotal. After completing my master's, I took time out to go sailing in the Caribbean and drew up a proposal for a PhD exploring the symbolism of colours in textile production in the Andes. But on the two month trip back over the Atlantic, I decided it was time for action. I would go back to Ecuador and put together a knitwear range with a cooperative I'd visited, using natural dyes and locally sourced buttons. My mum and friend chipped in £500 each for the flight and the production. Pachacuti (which means 'world upside-down', or 'the start of a new era' in Quechua) was about to be born.

Extraordinarily it all worked out, and I found myself, a few months later, coming back to England, with eighty pieces of knitwear that had cost £420 to produce. I took the collection to the Campus Arts Festival in Devon. It was 1992, the early days of glamping. I was in a four-person tent and totally unprepared. And it was a heat wave - who would want to buy sweaters?!

But that's what everyone else had thought as well. They were totally unprepared for the freezing cold evenings. Word got round, and there was a steady stream of campers coming to my tent. All eighty jumpers went, at £25 each.

Festivals seemed to be the place to sell. So I re-ordered, using the same cooperatives, picked up six boxes of sweaters from Heathrow, and headed for Greenbelt. It was the year of chunky knits and, as news had got out, there was a rush for my stand and the jumpers were being ripped out of the boxes as fast as I could unload them.

I managed to land a £5,000 loan, returned to Ecuador and rented a flat for a month. All seemed to be going really well. Until the flat was broken into, and every penny taken.

EMBRACING FAIR TRADE

ALL was not lost, however, even though Black Wednesday was shortly to follow, and the bank loan I was able to secure, backed up by my father, was at $1.30 to the £, rather than $2.00. But then I met a guy in a cafe, who had just inherited and gave me £1,000 in cash to help me get things back on track. Alan became my business partner for the next three years.

We added panama hats to our knitwear offer and it was the hats that were to become the core product, although I stuck with knitwear until 2012. I dropped knits, not because I lost interest, but as I couldn't afford the costs of separate auditing in another country (Bolivia), which would be needed to bring it into line with the hats which, by then, were accredited under the World Fair Trade Organisation Guarantee System.

It was in 2005, when I heard the WFTO was looking to introduce certification for fairly traded handicrafts, that I approached them. I wanted our panama hats to be the first product certified under the new scheme, as the panama had been such a symbol of colonial rule. For that reason, I thought it would be a great first fair trade product with the power of that symbol funnelled straight back into the hands of the producers.

The WFTO looked at all aspects of the business, from our internal social and environmental admin to quality control, to ensure that everything adhered to fair trade principals. The straw used in the hats could be traced back to where it was produced, the parcels of land where the straw was grown, testing for levels of bio-diversity, water used for processing, the energy used. And we were able to plan with the workers and their management, not just react when issues arose.

FASHION REVOLUTION

THE idea for Fashion Revolution came to me in the bath. It was just two days after the Rana Plaza garment factory collapse in Bangladesh, with 1,300 people killed and 2,500 injured. Yet, I have to confess, I was feeling just a little complacent and self-satisfied as I reflected that people would see why I had spent the previous three years ensuring traceability and transparency in every aspect of our supply chain.

With no podcast of the Archers - it was a Sunday evening - I had nothing to listen to. It was almost like a physical bolt that hit me. UNITE EVERYONE INTO A GLOBAL MOVEMENT TO COMMEMORATE THAT TRAGIC DAY.

If I hadn't had such experience of being entrepreneurial, as I got out of my bath, the idea may have floated down the plughole. Instead, I immediately phoned the person who had co-founded Estethica at London Fashion Week, Orsola de Castro. I didn't know Orsola that well at the time, but she was convinced immediately. Lucy Siegle called a couple of days later, and she was 100% behind the idea. The three of us sent a joint letter to some key contacts across the industry. The replies came flooding back: yes, yes, yes! We were determined that this tragedy should stand for something and everybody agreed.

The first Fashion Revolution Day was on 24th April 2014, twelve months to the day after the Rana Plaza collapse. The aim was to create a global movement of those who cared, all asking one question: "Who made my clothes?". By 2015, the campaign was in 81 countries, with 63 million people using #whomademyclothes, no. 1 trend on Twitter, and 16.5 billion global media reach in the month of April (20 billion for the year!)

WE WERE DETERMINED
THAT THIS TRAGEDY
SHOULD STAND
FOR SOMETHING ...
EVERYBODY AGREED

WHO MADE
MY CLOTHES?
www.fashionrevolution.org

PRESSING FOR CHANGE

IN December 2015, we published a White Paper; 'It's time for a Fashion Revolution'. The paper points towards specific actions that brands, retailers, suppliers, factories and wholesalers can take:

- operationalise an ethical code of conduct
- monitor, evaluate and report on social & environmental impact
- publish supply chain information
- map the supply chain right through to the farmer
- share photos and stories from across the supply chain
- report publicly about supply chain wages
- increase cost transparency to help consumers better understand where their money is going

'The Tipping Point' by Malcolm Gladwell is a key reference. In his book, published in 2000, Gladwell argues 'How Little Things Can Make a Big Difference', defining a tipping point as 'the moment of critical mass, the threshold, the boiling point'. 'Ideas, products, messages, behaviours spread like viruses ...' This is the principle we are following in Fashion Revolution.

We have to get to the point where, in the words of Orsola de Castro, fashion produced ethically and sustainably should just be called fashion. Everything else should be branded unethical fashion. Only then will we be able to feel that the tide is really turning.

We believe that 1,113 is too many people to lose from the planet in one factory, on one terrible day, to not stand up and demand change. We need a Fashion Revolution.

FROM HUMAN RIGHTS ABUSES AND POVERTY LEVEL WAGES TO WATER, WASTE, ENERGY OVERCONSUMPTION AND MANY OTHER EXPLOITATIVE PRACTICES, THE FASHION INDUSTRY IS IN DESPERATE NEED FOR TRANSFORMATIONAL, SYSTEMIC CHANGE

It's Time for a Fashion Revolution

The white paper can be found at: http://fashionrevolution.org/wp-content/uploads/2015/11/FashRev_Whitepaper_Dec2015_screen.pdf

---

FASHION PRODUCED ETHICALLY AND SUSTAINABLY SHOULD JUST BE CALLED FASHION. EVERYTHING ELSE SHOULD BE BRANDED UNETHICAL FASHION

Orsola de Castro

13

NOTHING TO WEAR

THE CRAZY PARADOX OF FAST FASHION

made
my
lothes?

#WHOMADEMYCLOTHES
FASHIONREVOLUTION.ORG

I have linked together the insatiable rise of fast fashion with the old adage that, in spite of a wardrobe full of clothes, "I have nothing to wear." I do this, as it seems to be a pretty universal truism that, the more we have of something, the more we want.

I'M LIKE EVERY OTHER WOMAN: A CLOSET FULL OF CLOTHES, BUT NOTHING TO WEAR

Cameron Diaz

Fast fashion is a term used to describe cheap and affordable clothes which are the result of catwalk designs moving into stores in the fastest possible way, in order to respond to the latest trends.

We have seen that the fast fashion retail model puts unmanageable pressure on the system, risking the health and safety of workers around the world, and threatening the very sustainability of our planet's resources and ecosystem. Surely, it also devalues our appreciation of the clothes we are wearing. Do we have the will to act?

Fashion Revolution is a global coalition of designers, academics, writers, business leaders and parliamentarians calling for systemic reform of the fashion supply chain.

FASHION REVOLUTION FOUNDER, CARRY SOMERS EXPLAINS:

WE want to use the power of fashion to inspire a permanent change in the fashion industry and reconnect the broken links in the supply chain. At the moment of purchase, most of us are unaware of the processes and impacts involved in the creation of a garment. We need to reconnect through a positive narrative, to understand that we aren't just purchasing a garment or accessory, but a whole chain of value and relationships.

By asking consumers, designers, brands, and all those who care to ask a simple question "Who Made My Clothes?" we envisage a change in perspective that will lead to a deeper understanding.

Be curious, find out, do something. Demand to know who are the individuals who makes your clothes and discover the organisations working on the field to make change happen.

BE CURIOUS
FIND OUT
DO SOMETHING
Carry Somers

ETHICS ON THE STREET

BERLINERS TAKE REVOLUTIONARY
FASHION CHALLENGE

24TH APRIL 2015 ... to draw attention to the terrible truth about how inexpensive clothing is produced, Fashion Revolution placed a vending machine in Alexanderplatz Square, Berlin, offering passers-by a t-shirt for only two euros. A surprise awaited them.

Once the patron put in the money and selected their size, the vending machine played a video about the conditions in the sweat shops where these kinds of clothes are made, including the abysmal pay and long hours without a break.

After twenty seconds of video, patrons were offered a choice: they could still choose to take the t-shirt, despite knowing the conditions they were made in, or they could choose to put the money toward Fashion Revolution, thereby helping to fight for better labour conditions and putting pressure on companies to be responsible for how their clothes are made.

image: fashionrevolution.org

DISPOSABLE CLOTHES THAT STAY IN A WOMAN'S CLOSET FOR AN AVERAGE OF JUST FIVE WEEKS, BEFORE BEING THROWN OUT
Livia Firth

BUY LESS, CHOOSE WELL
Vivienne Westwood

CONSUMERS NEED TO MAKE THE LINK BETWEEN THEIR DESIRE FOR CHEAP CLOTHING AND THE LOSS OF LIVELIHOODS THROUGH DEPLETED, POLLUTED FISHING STOCK AND EVER-DEPLETED FOOD AND WATER RESOURCES
Baroness Lola Young

WHEN A WOMAN SAYS "I HAVE NOTHING TO WEAR!" WHAT SHE REALLY MEANS IS "THERE'S NOTHING HERE FOR WHO I'M SUPPOSED TO BE TODAY"
Caitlin Moran

TRANSPARENCY IS KEY WHEN IT COMES TO SUSTAINABILITY. WE ARE A LUXURY BRAND AND LUXURY SETS THE TREND. IT'S OUR RESPONSIBILITY TO SHOW OTHERS THAT A SUSTAINABLE APPROACH IS NOT AN OPTION, BUT A NECESSITY
Tweet by Chief Sustainability Officer of a leading luxury group

SLOWING FASHION DOWN

TEN STEPS TOWARDS FASHION THAT
EMPOWERS RATHER THAN ENSLAVES

ANYONE working in fashion knows that it is like being on a hamster wheel - with a never ending cycle of new collections to design, produce, promote and sell. This relentlessness means that it has a tendency to ensnare and enslave both those producing and those consuming it, who seek to keep up with all this new product.

Husband and wife partnership, Az Henry and Josh Masih, consider this to be madness and are exploring biblical concepts to build an alternative model, SLOW-FASHION, that aims to create space to empower those making the clothes and to stimulate engagement for those wearing them, the customer.

Here, their "work-in-progress" thoughts are arranged into ten steps to challenge the hungry monster that is fast fashion.

AZLEEN HENRY & JOSHUA MASIH are visionary creative practitioners and academics. Having studied BA (Hons) Design Technology for the Fashion Industries: Menswear (Azleen) and Womenswear (Joshua), at the London College of Fashion, they gained industry experience at Alexander McQueen, Hardy Amies and high street retailer, Reiss before establishing their own company 'Paul Joshua Masih'. Both then held Senior Lectureship roles at the Arts University, Bournemouth for nine years and latterly at the London College of Fashion. They are looking to focus again on developing their own business, using principles they are naming 'Slow-Fashion'.

10 STEPS TO SLOW-FASHION

ETHICAL WORKING WEEK
- Monday to Thursday - Business
- Friday - Charity work
- Saturday & Sunday - Rest

ANNUAL SHOW
ONE show a year, fully immersing the audience in the world of the brand. Much like an artist, to make the impact of a presentation memorable.

POP-UP SHOPS
POP-UP shop for forty days, scheduled to balance with the annual show. Why forty days? Noah's life was transformed by forty days of rain; Moses was transformed by forty days on Mount Sinai; Jesus was empowered by forty days in the wilderness. Forty days seems to be a period that allows change to happen.

QR CODE
IDENTIFY and credit workers contributing to the design and manufacture of product through a Quick Response code printed on the label, swing tag and packaging.

SEVEN YEAR CYCLE
For six years you are to sow your fields and harvest the crops, but during the seventh year let the land lie unused and unploughed. Exodus 23: 10-11

CONSIDER working on Collections for six years, whilst investing in a programme of 'surplus' to provide for a year of creative expression during the seventh, during which there will be time to reflect and engage with God and people about the business, ready to explore without the boundaries set by the previous six years.

This unpacks the idea that when we rest, God works. On this premise, there is an opportunity for us to develop our faith, knowing that we don't need to work continuously. We can slow down to enjoy and reflect on particular set chapters in life.

RETAIL MODEL

A twin retail model, operating from the same digital platform that seeks to empower the individual and build a global community:

- Ready-to-wear products designed and manufactured with the ethical values that constitute the brand;

- Patterns purchased from the website and then printed out at home by the customer on a regular domestic printer.

EDUCATION

LEARNING + TEACHING. Each pattern purchased would be supported through a login and password to a range of videos and PDFs to aid the making of the products.

We would also continue with our lecturing to pass on our ideas and experience to a new generation of designers.

SOCIAL

AN added benefit of offering patterns is that, once the consumer has made the garment, there would be a portal to upload images and share with others, thereby becoming part of a creative community. This will empower the individual.

CORE SKILLS

FOCUSSING on the importance of core making skills is, in itself, a point of discussion: understanding that the digital era can and should be aligned with practical skills. Developing craft skills that become life long learning skills.

PRODUCTION

AIM to work in small teams. Continually networking with new small enterprises and factories, sharing 'good practices' and developing relationships.

QUALITY

DESIGNING and manufacturing products of excellence, by hand and machine. Taking time and consideration to explore each stage of the creative process, where those involved feel valued and skill sets are optimised through good practices. This would be under-pinned by limiting ourselves to one show per year.

IS THE IDEA OF SLOW-FASHION
JUST A PIPE DREAM?
Three questions for Az & Josh

WHY DID YOU PAUSE YOUR BUSINESS?

ONE of our projects was to produce a capsule collection for a high street retailer. With our background in tailoring, we tried to experiment with different approaches to our pattern cutting. But there simply wasn't time to do this. Everything was needed too quickly. We realised that it was not the right time for us to do what our hearts were telling us, so decided to move across to the academic world to share our tailoring, construction and fashion design skills with students.

WHY DO YOU FEEL THE TIME IS NOW RIGHT TO RETURN TO YOUR BUSINESS?

TIMES have moved on, and there is more interest today in clothes with individuality. We too have moved on. We understand better how our tailoring and fashion design skills can be used. Spiritually, we now have a clearer idea of what makes us tick and how we should be expressing what we believe through our approach to business. There is a market for fashion now that embraces good design married with ethical principles. Stepping out in faith, knowing that we have a mandate on our lives to demonstrate a way of exploring fashion creativity and innovation.

WHAT DO YOU SEE AS THE BENEFITS AND SACRIFICES OF A MORE 'RELAXED' APPROACH TO BUSINESS?

BE creative and explore processes at an organic pace. Find a business model that works for your lifestyle. The benefits are in exploring processes. The sacrifices are that it may take you longer to realise your productivity cycle. Reflect and explore, and learn from your mistakes to re-focus your business model. Our example is agriculture ... where humanity is learning that fresh and natural food makes for healthier living than processed, fast food. The same will be so for fashion. To re-educate ourselves to enjoy the experience of good design supported by ethical practice at every level. A new definition of luxury, that understands the value of quality, and has longevity to pass onto loved ones.

RE-PURPOSING UNIFORMS

WHAT BRINGS TOGETHER AN ONLINE SUPERMARKET, A PRISON IN
NORTHUMBERLAND AND A START-UP DESIGN COMPANY IN EAST LONDON?
THE ANSWER ... UNWANTED CORPORATE UNIFORMS

OCADO knew their uniforms were made of good quality material, but were aware that there was a high reputational risk if they ended up being available outside of the company. They contacted environmental charity, Hubbub, to seek ideas for a sustainable solution. A number of exploratory calls resulted in an unusual collaboration.

Everything in Colour is a new sustainable fashion brand dedicated to discovering creative uses for donated fabrics. It didn't take too long for them to re-purpose the uniforms into a range of products including tote bags, aprons, pet blankets and children's fluorescent safety jackets.

The next challenge was to find a way of making the new products in a cost-effective way. The solution was Northumberland Prison run by Sodexo.

The prison has a large textile facility which is part of their rehabilitation programme. They are constantly seeking manufacturing lines that give the prisoners skills and get them into a working routine. The uniforms fitted the bill perfectly.

The final piece of the jigsaw puzzle was to secure a market. Ocado's solution? Promote the products to their customers, using the income generated to support charities through their Foundation.

For Hubbub, the collaboration neatly creates environmental, social and financial benefit, but also prompted a look at the wider picture ... with surprising results.

Two in seven working people in the UK wear a uniform. Nearly 33 million corporate garments are provided for their use, and around 90% - 15,000 tonnes - goes to landfill or incineration each year. Concerns over security and brand protection, coupled with the complexities of recovering and de-branding uniforms, explain why so few are reused or recycled.

The Challenge is on!

Hubbub is a London based organisation seeking to make environmental matters matter across food, fashion, homes and neighbourhood, by creating fun and sociable campaigns.

www.hubbub.org.uk

ETHICAL FASHION
comment from Westminster
RT HON CAROLINE SPELMAN MP FOR MERIDIEN

HOW DID YOU BECOME INTERESTED IN SUSTAINABLE FASHION?

WHEN I was Secretary of State for the Environment, at first I thought 'sustainable fashion' was an oxymoron, as fashion is by nature ever-changing and new, whereas sustainability refers to re-using and recycling materials. But the more I learnt about the burgeoning ecological fashion movement, the more I was excited by it. I was not the only person to think a little more about the contents of my wardrobe after the Rana Plaza tragedy. When we often pay so little for our clothing, it is hardly surprising that they are not produced in an environmentally sustainable manner, nor are the workers in the clothing factories paid a proper wage or employed in proper working conditions.

I am glad that many of the high street brands, producing in factories like Rana Plaza, have committed to check their supply chains to root out modern-day slavery (as it is commonplace for children and adults to be employed on a pittance, stuck in a spiral of indentured servitude) and to encourage sustainable manufacturing.

In the UK, innovative designers are leading the way by showing how effective recycled materials can be, when creating new designs. Christopher Raeburn uses parachute silks to create beautiful dresses, and breathes new life into WW2 army trench coats, so they can be worn in the 21st century. 'Green fashion' has been adopted by big brands such as Topshop, which demonstrates that consumers have a great deal of power. We can use our wallets to demonstrate that working conditions in clothing factories and ecological production influences our spending patterns.

WHAT CAN CENTRAL GOVERNMENT DO TO STIMULATE CHANGE?

National companies, such as Veolia, are ensuring their uniforms are produced from recycled textiles and the re-purposing of corporate uniforms is something on which Government can bring specific influence to bear. The Modern Slavery Act 2015 is a landmark showing that Government takes ethical issues seriously. It is tempting, though, to think that Government can wave a legislative wand to put everything right on the international front. The recent climate change talks showed that this is a long and complex process. Nevertheless, industry and Government must work closely together to address challenges and assess opportunities to speeden the day when ethical fashion is the norm.

RT HON CAROLINE SPELMAN was Environment Secretary from 2010-12 and Co-Chair of the All-Party Parliamentary Group on Ethics and Sustainability in Fashion. Caroline is Second Church Estates Commissioner and Patron of the Conservative Christian Fellowship.

171

WHEN DOES 'SKINNY' BECOME 'TOO SKINNY' ... AND SET AN IMPOSSIBLE IDEAL?

ALTHOUGH THIN MODELS ARE NOT THE CAUSE OF EATING DISORDERS, THEY CAN BE A TRIGGER OR A FACTOR IN MAINTAINING AN EATING DISORDER
Susan Albers, Cleveland Clinic

NOTHING TASTES AS GOOD AS SKINNY FEELS
Kate Moss

VOGUE.CO.UK tweet 10.02.16 ...
We are calling time on skinny jeans, will you give up yours this season?

IN 2006, two South American fashion models died in quick succession from causes linked to eating disorders. An international media storm blew up over what was dubbed 'The Size Zero debate', and the hounds were set running in pursuit of the fashion industry for promoting unhealthy ideals of body size.

The finger was particularly pointed at 'skinny models' walking the world's catwalks, and the spotlight was initially trained on Body Mass Index, a height/weight ratio that some insisted was the best measure of whether a model was healthy or not. A number of organisations running fashion weeks around the world were quick to ban models with a BMI under 18.5 ... and that, pretty much, was the last we heard of their efforts.

At the British Fashion Council, we decided not to jump on the bandwagon for London Fashion Week, recognising that we couldn't effect meaningful change to such a big issue by a knee jerk reaction. We chose to approach the matter carefully, identifying an effective and deliverable course of action that would protect the models, our first priority, and also help move things forward on a broader front where it was in our power to do so.

An Inquiry was set up, chaired by Baroness Denise Kingsmill, a member of the House of Lords with considerable experience of addressing high profile and controversial issues. Substantial background research was carried out, including a visit to the Priory Clinic in south west London to discuss the causes of eating disorders and the relevance of BMI as a measure of health. Some key findings from the Kingsmill Inquiry are set out below.

- models under the age of sixteen should be banned from the catwalks at London Fashion Week

- a healthy backstage environment at London Fashion Week is a priority, with drug-free venues and good quality food

- a health education and awareness programme for models should be established

- industry consideration of a voluntary code governing the use of digital manipulation

At the time of writing, a law is being introduced in France making provision of health certificates by all models a legal requirement. Exactly how this might work in practice, and whether it will help to protect models and address unhealthy ideals of body image, remains to be seen.

A POWERFUL VOICE …

THE issue, however, runs much wider than models. In the words of Steven Kolb, CEO of the Council of Fashion Designers of America, "Fashion Week has become a powerful voice, which reaches millions of people across the globe and we should not underestimate the consequences of the messages that we send."

Susan Albers, a psychologist at the Cleveland Clinic, explains: "Although thin models are not the cause of eating disorders, they can be a trigger or a factor in maintaining an eating disorder," In other words, if a woman has a predis-position for an eating disorder and spends a lot of time looking at fashion magazines, this can be one of the factors that triggers feeling bad about her body, which she then turns into eating disorder behaviour, like excessive dieting." (*Huffington Post, Sept 2013*)

And then there is the matter of digital manipulation of images in fashion magazines, an issue that was to come to the forefront in 2003, as the actress Kate Winslet protested when radically changed images of her appeared in a UK magazine, whose editor commented: *"almost no picture that appears … has not been digitally altered in some way."*

Has the fashion industry taken the view that it is acceptable to ignore the impact it has on millions of 'normal' people who aspire to, but will never achieve, the ideals placed before them?

A MODEL'S EYE ON IMAGE

CHRISTINA NEARMAN

EATING disorders take more lives than all the other mental illnesses, and are a growing issue - from children through adults, males and females. The underlying roots, which propel these disordered eating behaviours into dangerous and life-taking habits and illness, are still not completely clear, including the role and impact of body image. Much of the focus seems to be on anorexia and the ideals of attaining an emaciated body, which is often blamed on the influence of the fashion industry. However, in the general population, binge eating disorder, taking in large amounts of food at one sitting, affects around two-thirds of all those with eating disorders. Whilst eating disorders continue taking the lives of people of all shapes and sizes, genders and ethnicities, and both malnutrition and obesity put an incredible strain on the body, the main message has been to eliminate the 'thin-ideal', for women in particular.

Within the fashion industry, body-size is also tricky, as many entering the fashion model profession have naturally slimmer frames. Whilst it is necessary to develop guidelines and laws to protect models, a BMI limit, to avoid unhealthily thin models from gaining employment, may also strip the means of earning a living, for those who are not able to gain weight easily (in their natural state). Just as some naturally have a more overweight tendency and body shape, there are others who naturally have the opposite issue. I will never forget a fashion model from South America in tears, as frequent rude and mean comments were made about her body size, and under her social media photos. Coming from a culture where curvy is the ideal body type for women, and her very slim natural body type, she always desired and tried to gain more weight.

Therefore, we must consider all the different shapes and sizes, in our attitudes, comments, and in how to protect both the industry professionals and the public. A larger, curvier body, as well as a very slim body does not make someone more or less a 'real' woman, or cause more or less suffering from disordered eating. Rude comments and assumptions are not acceptable whether someone is under-weight or overweight. Messages that someone is not 'enough', 'real', or 'worthy' because of their size and shape - should not be acceptable. Instead, we must all work to develop an embracing society, which cheers on others' beauty, gifts and talents, while also cheering on our own.

CHRISTINA NEARMAN, a former model and now the International Director of gModa (see section 4), has an MSc in Neuro-Imaging and Neuro-Clinical Psychology, and is currently working on a PhD, using neuro-imaging techniques to research the implicit underlying mechanisms of eating disorders.

WE should each contribute to reducing a spirit of competitiveness and meanness, especially relating to outer appearance. It is also important to research the facts behind these issues, so that we may develop the most effective safeguard.

That is why my focus is investigating these underlying roots, so that my research may help develop prevention and treatments which are more effective and save lives - both within fashion and throughout the world.

BATTLING WITH MY BODY

JENNAVAVE BARBERO SHARES HER EXPERIENCE OF ANOREXIA & BULIMIA ... AND SUGGESTS SOME WARNING SIGNS

HAVING lived on both sides of eating disorders, I have experienced losing a healthy balance. Before I was a model, I was a healthy, athletic teen with no cares about what I ate, either before, during or after meals. It never entered my mind. I did sports, I got hungry, I ate, I enjoyed it ... and didn't experience guilt or shame. I was totally free.

When I became a model, I was told I had to lose weight off my hips. I was very methodical about it. I calculated how many calories a day I had to burn. No one guided me. I just did what I thought was what was required of me. I was barely fifteen. After months of following an extreme dietary regimen, and doing aerobic exercise every day, the pangs of anorexia began.

Though I met my goal, I lost my innocent relationship with food. I saw only numbers, as if each food item had a calorie bubble hovering over it ... the ding ding ding of my mental calorie register never stopped. Food wasn't about nourishing my body, nor was it about enjoyment. It became an adversary. I had begun a vicious downward spiral of mental trickery that denied my

body what it needed and ignored its impulses. My emotions became imbalanced, as I grew ever more fixated on my measurements. Suddenly, looking at my body became something of a sordid, daily ritual.

I lost my innocent relationship to my own body. Any perceived additional flesh was disgusting to me. I would stand in front of the mirror, pinch my thigh muscles, and mentally tell myself it was all fat that had to be eliminated. I began to suffer body dysmorphia, literally believing I could see my body getting fat in front of me.

I lost the ability to see reality, as my own eyes betrayed me. Eating became a horrifying experience where my fear of getting fat increased with each bite, and seeing others eat was enough to make me feel nausea.

When my hunger cravings became too strong, I began to cave in. I flipped from anorexic tendencies to bulimic. I would suffer voracious binges late in the night and early morning, hiding it from my parents, and I would eat until I couldn't eat any more ... until I wanted to throw up.

JENNAVAVE BARBERO is a designer, former model, and major catalyst for redefining beauty in the fashion industry. She leads the Milan-based branch of gModa.

175

AND I wanted to throw up ... to release the stress and pressure. I would lie in bed in agony, sweating as my body tried to process the flood of food, lying on my side, because every other position hurt my overstuffed abdomen.

I didn't sleep well at all. Many times I tried to make myself vomit, but knowing what that meant, prevented me. I didn't want to admit I was bulimic. Instead I would spend hours and hours in the gym the next day, killing myself, trying to burn off the calories I had consumed the night before. Somehow that, for me, was more healthy, but my reasoning and caloric calculations at that point were far from healthy.

My self-esteem was hanging on every word I heard around me. I had given my power, the power of knowing who I was, away to the opinions of others - opinions often offered without an ounce of care, and even with cruelty. The dread of having to be measured in front of everyone, was a huge motivator for avoiding (at all cost) being called fat, but the utter humiliation, when the feedback was not flattering, was pure torture.

All day long, casting after casting, agents and photographers - they all had their own opinions, and they were all different. What to believe!? What is the truth?

Fittings, go-sees and designers, everyone has a different ideal of beauty. A size 6 became a size 4, then a 2; and then zero ... where does it all end? When does skinny become too skinny?

PRs, bookers and scouts are full of suggestions and career advice. Where am I safe? Where do I belong? Should I really go to that party?

And bulimia is not sustainable. I ended up in hospital on an IV, because I had repeated this cycle so much, that I had severely dehydrated my body.

Desperate to find a way around my hunger problem, I discovered that doing ecstasy eliminated any desire to eat food. So a little of that, a large dose of mental treachery, an excess of gym activity and, with any luck, the recipe would work. But no, it didn't. The situation got worse, before it got better.

Then, at a certain point, I had an epiphany, a spiritual intervention. I was allowed to see myself from a celestial perspective, where I could see the destination of the road I was on. I was literally killing myself, and I was losing my very identity. I was approaching the point of no return.

For all my chasing of some world view of beauty, I was destroying my own, and becoming something ugly. I made one of the most difficult decisions I ever had to make, but it was the right one.

I decided my health was more important; that my dignity was priceless; that my identity was more than skin; and that my soul could be happy doing something else.

That was when I began a long road to recovery from fear and shame and, thank God, today I am wiser and free once again.

EATING DISORDER WARNING SIGNS

IF you absolutely must count the calories, don't be fooled - there is a problem. It is obsessive behaviour - a sure sign of a dependency which is rooted in fear. Deal with the fear.

CAN you pass a mirror without sneaking a glimpse? Do you see reality? If the mirror is like a magnet to you, it may not just be vanity. Eating disorders are accompanied by an almost uncontrollable urge to control weight and hyper-analyse the body.

ARE you hyper-aware of your posture, - holding in your stomach, for example? If you can't be in company without the tension of trying to give them the best angle, you've got the onset of insecurity.

IF you feel guilty, be sure the reason is sane. Eating a pint of gelato after a full dinner may merit some guilt, but it serves to help us keep balance. However, there is no shame in eating a healthy plate of veggies and a breast of chicken for lunch.

DO you get nervous about food consumption? Eating food should not cause a precondition of anxiety.

IF eating food has lost its enjoyment, do all you can to find it again. Food, and the experience of eating it, is supposed to stimulate pleasure, and this helps our system to digest and absorb the nutrients properly.

SKIPPING meals is a mild introduction to eating disorders, which are psychosomatic in nature. It's a slippery slope, and it's not worth it. Besides, not eating regularly causes imbalances with your metabolism.

IF you often say things like, "oh, I forgot to eat", but deep down you know you ignored your body's messages, you're playing with fire. This is classic anorexic behaviour.

IF you look at a menu with a no-fat, no-carb, 'no-calorie' filter, you have lost your innocent relationship with food. The same is true if you say you are vegan or allergic to 'everything' to hide an extreme diet. Being aware and wise about your nutrition needs is important. The body needs both fat and carbs.

IF you cannot eat without thinking about how much - and think you'll need to run to burn it off - things are out of balance. Eating food should never trigger an impulse to go burn it off.

IF you develop a hatred for overweight people, or an insensitivity and judgmental reaction to obesity, it is a fear-based obsession that needs to be put in check.

IF the dining experience, and seeing others eat, becomes something you cannot stand to see, then consider that you may be suffering from self-loathing.

IF you find you can't stop eating, then start satisfying your heart's appetite for healthy, non-selfish loving relationships, first of all with yourself. That's where the real imbalance comes from.

For help on Eating Disorders: in the UK, you can contact BEAT: Adult (over 18) Helpline: 0345 634 1414; email: help@b-eat.co.uk. Youthline (u25): 0345 634 7650; email:fyp@b-eat.co.uk. In The USA, contact NEDA's confidential Helpline: 1-800-931-2237

A NEW STYLE CULTURE?

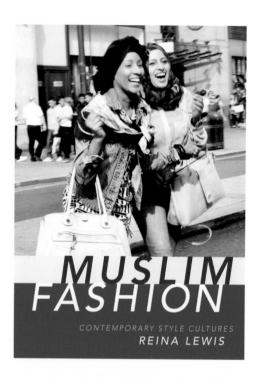

MUSLIM
FASHION

CONTEMPORARY STYLE CULTURES
REINA LEWIS

MOST PEOPLE SEEMED TO VIEW
AS CONTRADICTORY THE FACT
THAT I WAS TRYING TO PUT
RELIGION AND FASHION IN
THE SAME FRAME

WHAT would have been deemed appropriate and inappropriate dress in past generations is very different to today - whether the cut of the clothing, or the manner and extent to which it covers the body. I will not, here, be considering the pros and cons of any particular view or, indeed, whether this is anyone's business other than the wearer's.

However, in the Bible, the apostle Paul, in one of the pastoral letters to his young friend Timothy, advises that it is appropriate for those under his care to dress with 'modesty, decency and propriety'. This remains important to many religions today.

Professor Reina Lewis was principal investigator on *Faith-based Fashion and Internet Retail*, a research project exploring the growing market for modest clothing among women of the three Abrahamic faiths: Islam, Judaism and Christianity. She is author of *Muslim Fashion: Contemporary Style Cultures* and editor of *Modest Fashion: Styling Bodies, Mediating Faiths*.

Reina shares some of the background to her work, particularly amongst Muslim women in Britain. The research gives insight for anyone interested in dressing with modesty, yet with an eye to fashion.

WHY DOES MODEST FASHION INTEREST YOU?

MY research in this area began after 9/11 and the 2005 London bombings, when images of women wearing 'Muslim' clothes were all over the media, within an alarmist framework that presented Muslims as a potential threat to western security - as if Muslims themselves weren't part of the West and weren't equally under threat themselves. I despaired of this, particularly in light of earlier work I had done about gender and orientalism and the way in which gender identities are racialised and racial identities are gendered and class specific.

But, I also saw that something else was going on: a new style culture, with cool young hijabis everywhere I looked. Yet this was never celebrated as part of British street style.

REINA LEWIS is Professor of Cultural Studies at the London College of Fashion, UAL. Her specialisms include Fashion and Faith, especially internet retail, blogs and magazines; Fashion and Islam, especially historical and contemporary veiling debates; critical approaches to Orientalism, especially travel writing, photography, and Orientalist painting; Middle Eastern and Ottoman women's history (1800-1945); postcolonial theory, gender and ethnicity/race studies; Sexuality studies, including lesbian and gay visual and literary culture, queer fashion, queer theory; retail geographies and non-western modernities.

WHAT LAY BEHIND THIS NEW STYLE CULTURE?

I saw that increasing numbers of younger women were electing to wear a headscarf, for many different reasons: some because of personal devotion and piety; some to assuage family concerns - a guarantee of respectability; some because the hijab had become a sign of stigma, and they wanted to transform it, through style, to something positive.

Muslim women have been dressing modestly in accordance with their understanding of holy texts and community convention for generations. What was new, here, was that this generation was doing it through their own choice and by participating in mainstream consumer culture, mixing 'traditional' or 'ethnic' dress with clothes and accessories from the high street.

The strapline for my book could have been 'Muslim fashion: over-represented in the news media, underrepresented in the style media.' Most people seemed to view as contradictory the fact that I was trying to put religion and fashion in the same frame. Putting Muslim women and fashion together was even more so.

> MOST PEOPLE SEEMED TO VIEW AS CONTRADICTORY THE FACT THAT I WAS TRYING TO PUT RELIGION AND FASHION IN THE SAME FRAME

WERE YOU SEEING SOMETHING MORE THAN A FASHION STATEMENT?

THERE was something political going on – youngsters were using fashion to challenge stereotypes about Muslims. In my work I wanted to de-exceptionalise young Muslims, because it was clear that challenges to wider presumptions that faith was incompatible with fashion were coming from other faith groups too.

And not only those who affiliated formally to a religion… I would also include the increasing number of people who are interested in religion and belief in a broadest sense; it is not only about belonging to a church, a mosque, a syngaogue. A lot of people define themselves as spiritual, not religious, and this provides the framework for their interaction with the world. How they dress and present themselves can be a key part of that.

> THIS IS A YOUTHFUL POPULATION … THEY DON'T NECESSARILY SEE CONSUMER CULTURE AS SOMETHING OPPOSITIONAL TO THEIR EXPRESSION OF RELIGIOUS IDENTITIES

This is a youthful population, who've grown up with world music, world food, world fashion, and they don't necessarily see consumer culture as something oppositional to their expression of religious identities.

In Britain, expression of modest fashion is predominantly amongst young Muslims, with smaller numbers of Jews and Christians involved. But you look at North America, it is Christian and Jewish communities that form the largest sectors of modest fashion activity.

CHOICES

THE women I spoke to emphasised that they were choosing to wear hijab. They would argue, very clearly, that if you impose it, that would be wrong. Likewise, if you force someone to uncover, that also would be wrong. In Britain, there are Muslim women who are unable to exercise much choice in whether, when and how to uncover. But there is also a sizeable number who are able to choose.

HIJAB - IF YOU IMPOSE IT, THAT WOULD BE WRONG. LIKEWISE, IF YOU FORCE SOMEONE TO UNCOVER, THAT ALSO WOULD BE WRONG

All of us, of course, are subject to surveillance and regulation about what we can and can't wear, dependant on a wide range of factors, such as age, occupation and the space we are in. For many of the young women I spoke to, of all religious backgrounds, rights to self-defined religious expression are seen as part of human rights.

In terms of how women achieve modest fashion, there are generational and micro-generational distinctions. So, clothes a women might wear aged eighteen, are likely to be very different to when she is twenty-eight and thirty-eight.

IT'S partly down to how individual women interpret the requirements of modest dress and behaviour within their own faith community. Those interpretations will be historically specific, and will likely change over time and the course of their own lives.

A DEFINITION OF 'MODEST'?

As we've briefly considered, what a woman considers modest at eighteen will certainly be different to when they are forty. It's the same for everybody. It's important not to see Muslim women as emblems of a collective a-historical group or essentialised cultural identity, as if they are not part of modern society. Fashion is a way of communicating that they are part of modern Britain, or western culture.

FASHION IS A WAY OF COMMUNICATING BEING PART OF THE SAME PRESENT

For designers or brands, the term 'modest' can be the kiss of death when dealing with the mainstream fashion industry, because it can sound too limiting, prudish, self-abnegating and restrictive. Modesty is sometimes on trend, such as when Kate Middleton's wedding dress made her the pin up girl for modest fashion. But then it goes off the fashion agenda, and is relegated again to the zone of unfashionable.

ANTI-FASHION AND AESTHETICS

THERE is a strand of anti-fashion in Muslim and modest dressing. Go back to the mid 20th century, and the early piety movements embraced simple homemade clothes or those made by local seamstresses. It was a way of being against fashion, capitalism or a show of social status.

Fast forward, and we now have a generation immersed in global fashion cultures. Young women finding ways to adapt global trends to meet their modesty needs.

There is no single aesthetic. Modest fashion can look different in different countries, but a niche market has emerged, mainly women-led from within particular faith communities - which the internet and blogging has allowed to develop as images transfer transnationally and new style cultures emerge.

WE NOW HAVE A GENERATION IMMERSED IN GLOBAL FASHION CULTURES. YOUNG WOMEN FINDING WAYS TO ADAPT GLOBAL TRENDS TO MEET THEIR MODESTY NEEDS

shop assistant styling headscarf on mannequin in-store, Tuğba & Venn, Fatih, Istanbul, 2009
photo: Reina Lewis

MODEST IS THE HOTTEST
STRENGTH FROM MODESTY

MITH is a new magazine, with a focus on modest fashion. It's co-founder, Holly Glasser, explains:

WE strive to give our readers fashion and entertainment role models to look up to who are tastefully elegant, helping women develop their identity and worth from within, as opposed to placing excessive emphasis on flaunting oneself for outward approval.

MITH stands for Modest Is The Hottest, and is also an old Celtic word meaning 'strength'.

We are a movement and a lifestyle that seeks to raise up a generation of strong individuals in arts and entertainment who are leaders, entrepreneurs, pioneers and philanthropists, showcasing inner beauty and strength as more important than outward beauty. While not detracting from outward beauty and appearance, we simply condone fashion that is tasteful and elegant to match the soul's truer purpose.

Indeed, our magazine is geared towards a woman who is seeking fulfillment and inspiration through creativity, innovation, and helping those around her, while epitomizing what it means to be a true 'lady'. In this way, we hope to rebalance the fashion and entertainment industry by telling stories that cultivate modest beauty in a positive way that is soul nourishing and ultimately fulfilling on a deeper level. We seek to do all this while still bringing top-of-the-line fashion that is both inspiring, eye-catching, and invigorating, bringing meaning and bliss to the readers of MITH.

www.mithmagazine.com

TALENT ... OR WHO YOU KNOW?

DURING my years working in fashion, I've often heard the throw away line *"it's not what you know, but who you know"* that gets you a job in fashion.

There's some truth in this, particularly at the higher end of the industry. But it can't be the best way, unless it's just your friends who have talent! No, talent is spread through the population, and some would argue that creative talent is more likely to be found in those less well connected, as they will have to fall back on their raw gifts rather than educated polish. Certainly some of the leading British designers came from backgrounds that were far from well off.

A key to 'getting into fashion' is to know just what careers are available. Many think that the choice is restricted to becoming a designer or stepping out as a model and maybe being a retail buyer. And that, therefore, you either have to go to University and rack up a colossal debt, or be extremely tall!

Not so. There is a huge range of careers with access through apprenticeships, university or just getting straight in there.

A word of warning - fashion, like the other creative industries, is not the place to work if you are not prepared to roll up your sleeves and give it your best shot.

HAVE I GOT TALENT?
turn the page for an expert's top 10 indicators

FASHION IS NOT
THE PLACE TO WORK
IF YOU ARE NOT
PREPARED TO ROLL
UP YOUR SLEEVES
AND GIVE IT
YOUR BEST SHOT

for careers in fashion, check out:
www.britishfashioncouncil.com

FIRST STEPS? The British Fashion Council, at the time of writing, is working with the Sorrell Foundation to pilot Saturday Clubs for fashion *(www.saturday-club.org)*. These are targetted at school-aged young people, running every Saturday morning for thirty weeks a year and will give a great introduction to the range of careers in the industry with hands on experience and inspiring master classes.

There is nothing to beat a Saturday job working in a shop to see how fashion works. You engage with a wide range of product and consumers, and get insight into what works and what doesn't.

The Fashion Retail Academy gives an excellent and inspiring introduction to the world of fashion.
(www.fashionretailacademy.ac.uk)

Apprenticeships used to have a bit of a reputation - bricklayers or hairdressers - but a new wave of opportunities are opening up, including the Fashion Studio Assistant apprenticeship.
(www.creativeskillset.co.uk/fashion)

THE TALENT CHAMPION

IS BRITAIN'S FASHION TALENT AT RISK?

image: Alex Bramall

SARAH MOWER MBE

One of the world's leading fashion journalists, a critic for US Vogue and advocate for young designers, Sarah is the British Fashion Council's Ambassador for Emerging Talent and Chair of its New Gen committee, the scheme responsible for the rise of a constellation of design stars who show at London Fashion Week. A trustee of the British Fashion Council Education Foundation, Sarah is a passionate campaigner, raising scholarships for the students who will contribute to the health of the industry's future in all its developing areas.

THE ABOLITION OF
THE OLD ART SCHOOL
SYSTEM CAUSED THE
PROLIFERATION OF
MANY COURSES
WHICH ARE NOT
FIT FOR PURPOSE

A GOLDEN AGE OF FASHION TALENT ...

DURING the first decade of this Century, London saw the emergence of a 'Golden Age' of fashion design talent. Designers including Jonathan Saunders, Roksanda Ilincic, Erdem, Nicholas Kirkwood, JW Anderson, Christopher Kane, Christopher Raeburn, Mary Katrantzou and Simone Rocha studied at Britain's world class fashion colleges and were supported through their early years in business as New Generation designers.

Never in history had such a strong and varied cohort of British fashion companies risen to a position where they were exporting round the world, contributing to UK GDP and creating employment by manufacturing in the UK.

There was no better measure of this than the fact that global fashion groups, at a time when mergers and acquisitions were in the air, descended on London, competitively 'shopping' for their corporate futures.

Yet, many of the up and coming generation are struggling. Why?

... AT RISK?

THE majority of the members of this golden cohort of designers, who are now international names, benefitted from passing through UK fashion education when higher education was free or affordable.

In 2010, the cap on English university fees was removed with fees tripling to £9,000. By 2011, with the rise in student debt, only one English student was part of New Generation, which comprised mainly ex-International, British educated students: JJS Lee (Korean), Lucas Nascimento (Brazilian) and Paula Gerbase (Brazilian).

Then, in 2012, the UK government abolished two-year extension visas for International students, who are now being sent home before they can contribute to British GDP.

Meanwhile, university fashion department budgets are being cut, student numbers swelled by international intake, and standards of excellence eroded. In tandem with this, the abolition of the old art school system caused the proliferation of many courses which are not fit for purpose - if their purpose is to feed the needs of the industry.

HAVE I GOT TALENT?

SARAH MOWER'S TOP 10 INDICATORS

WHAT DID YOU PLAY WITH WHEN YOU WERE A CHILD?
I'VE learned to ask this question of all the new talent I come across – and the successful and established ones, too. The answers are always delightfully revealing, because all creative people, and the ones who help them in business, always started by dressing their dolls and teddy-bears, or making paper cutout dolls, or making mini-sets out of cardboard, playing fashion shows, cutting up clothes and dressing up, sticking pictures all over their bedroom walls, putting on performances for their families, selling tickets to families and neighbours to come and see them, and playing shop. I have concluded that this is always the way that imagination and entrepreneurship starts. This is no different from being a future athlete, sportsperson, engineer, scientist, writer, musician or artist. Encouraging children's play is the most important thing we can do. Playing with Barbies has had an enormous, underestimated effect on the fashion industry!

HOW HARD DO YOU CONCENTRATE?
ONE of the vital indicators for talent is being able to concentrate on one thing and keeping at it. Usually that comes from loving whatever it is – sometimes it can seem like a 'hobby' or something you don't do or learn in school. I realised the truth of this when I read Malcolm

Gladwell's book 'Outliers: The Story of Success' in which he analyses data about the backgrounds of successful people in business, tech and sport. All of them practiced 10,000 hours before they even started to compete in their jobs. That sounds scary, but childhood 'practise' in play absolutely counts in this (see 1.) - so you may well have been studying far longer than you think.

DO YOU HAVE YOUR OWN WORLD WITHIN YOU?
FASHION relies on new people coming in with new ideas – it is in a constant state of revolution, and it needs visionaries. What it doesn't need is people who just do the same as everyone else. I have learned to look for creative people who have strong ideas which are personal to them. Often, getting to those ideas just means being very honest about what you like and believe in, and having the courage to stick to it, even going against teachers if they don't see it.

HOW CURIOUS ARE YOU?
RESEARCHING and going out to look at as many things as you possibly can – galleries, museums, libraries – it all counts. Successful people in all branches of fashion have built up an encyclopaedic knowledge of the history of everything in whatever field obsesses them. You can find things out on the internet, but that's just a beginning.

CAN YOU MAKE THINGS?

ONE of the down-sides of the computer age is that people are growing up thinking that everything can just be designed on a screen, and then somehow clothes and accessories are just spat out of a machine at the end. No! Producing things to wear is a physical process. Developing a skill and thinking around the problems of how to make things matters. Designers who start by fitting their clothes on a real person have a vast head-start – the human body isn't theory! Sketching, painting, collaging, keeping notebooks also count. Discovering that you like pattern-cutting can lead to a great career in its own right. The fashion industry needs people with real skills who are creative problem-solvers.

WHAT JOBS HAVE YOU DONE?

SUPPORTING yourself in a very expensive world is getting harder than ever, so it's likely that every student today needs to work as well as study. If there's a choice, I recommend working in a fashion store or business, whatever it is, at whatever level. Working with clothes and people has many advantages and can be a form of study and research in itself. What sells? What doesn't? What do customers say about the clothes? What are they looking for that they don't find? Do the managers know how to respond to customers? How are the clothes made? Do they fit? You can learn so much from real experience in all these things – and it might lead you in many different directions which wouldn't be visible to you otherwise.

ARE YOU DYSLEXIC?

GREAT! It's a fact that the gift of extreme visual talent very often comes with dyslexia. I learned this when I was made a Fellow of the Royal College of Art. I sat next to an academic at the graduation ceremony at the Royal Albert Hall, which was filled with people who were receiving their Masters Degrees in fashion, fine art, ceramics, graphics, architecture, textiles, product and car design. He whispered to me: "Do you realise that three quarters of the people in this room are dyslexic?"

HAVE YOU GOT YOUR PEOPLE AROUND YOU?

THE successful independent designers of the last decade have all come in pairs. Even if they appear to be a single genius, there's always someone with them behind the scenes – sisters, brothers, boyfriends, girlfriends, schoolfriends, mothers, dads. Getting things done in fashion means being able to get other people to help. Forming a gang and taking collective action using lots of different talent is the way to get on, and get noticed, no matter how young you are. Friends and family are always the best moral supporters too – obviously!

ARE YOU PATIENT?

HARDLY anyone shoots to instant success in fashion – and even if they do, they will still face unexpected hurdles. There will be plenty of set-backs, disappointments, and problems to overcome, as there always are in life. Getting all the experience you can, will do you good in the long run – and you might discover other open doors you never imagined along the way. It's not a race.

IS THIS YOUR LIFE?

ONE thing to know about being in fashion is that there's practically no nine-to-five. Fashion and fashion people work at an incredibly fast pace, and often for very long hours. Despite all the hard work you have to enjoy it so much that you just can't imagine doing anything else.

SHOULD WE BE PAYING OUR YOUNG PEOPLE?

A lot of ink has been spilled, banners waved and fingers pointed in the ongoing debate about unpaid internships. There are two sides to the argument.

On the one hand, young people need experience, but will not be able to contribute a huge amount straight away. Businesses, particularly smaller ones, won't get a great deal of value from interns and will need to allocate resources to support them. From a practical point of view, many smaller start up businesses desperately need help to survive, yet do not have the financial resources to pay interns.

On the other hand, interns have to live! So you are restricting yourselves, either to those nearby who can live at home, or to those wealthy enough not to worry about being paid. Hardly the best catchment. And then, you don't value what you don't pay for, so many interns find themselves treated like the slaves they effectively are, even though they are doing the same work as paid staff.

Somewhat conclusively, the view of HMRC (the tax man) is that, if you are in the market for work (ie. not in education or training) and are doing work (regardless of any title you might be given) you should be paid as a worker - at least at the National Minimum Wage. So not paying interns is illegal. Whoever you are, and however much people want to work for you. Period.

What are the options? What is the 'right thing'?

At the British Fashion Council, we did several things to respond:

1. Advised everyone that unpaid interns were illegal.

2. Recommended more structured use of student work placements, ideally with expenses and some payment, even if modest.

3. Set up an apprenticeship scheme for school leavers.

4. Extended our scholarship programme to help less well off students at university.

5. Piloted a funded traineeship scheme for graduates.

There are now better structured and supported options, both for students and companies.

And the right thing? Surely any industry needs to invest in the upcoming generation. It will rarely be easy, but without it, the sector will stagnate, fade and die.

SIMON WARD worked for the British Fashion Council for thirty years, latterly as Chief Operating Officer, when he led discussions with HMRC about unpaid internships and oversaw the creation of the first fashion studio apprenticeship and a programme to help those exploring careers in fashion.

image: Shaun James Cox

THE WHOLE POINT OF AN
INTERNSHIP IS THAT IT ISN'T
A JOB - IT'S AN OPPORTUNITY.
SO IT MAKES PERFECT SENSE
THAT THERE'S NO PAY PACKET
AT THE END OF THE WEEK
Journalist, UK magazine

PERSONAL CONNECTIONS
RATHER THAN TALENT ARE
THE DECIDING FACTORS IN
WHETHER PEOPLE GET ON
British MP

IN THE NAME OF GAINING
EXPERIENCE, I HAVE DONE
JOBS THAT A PAID EMPLOYEE
WOULD OTHERWISE BE
ASKED TO DO
Student

MY UNPAID INTERNSHIP WAS
THE BEST THING THAT EVER
HAPPENED TO ME
Editorial Director, NY magazine

I PAY MY INTERNS SO I GET
THE BEST TALENT, NOT JUST
THOSE WHO CAN AFFORD
NOT TO BE PAID
UK Editor-in-Chief

ANY INDUSTRY NEEDS TO
INVEST IN THE UPCOMING
GENERATION. IT WILL RARELY
BE EASY, BUT WITHOUT IT,
THE SECTOR WILL STAGNATE,
FADE AND DIE

FASHION is not alone in its long hours culture. Workers in the UK are at their work stations longer than many of their European counterparts. Americans take it a step further, with a long working hours culture compounded by taking significantly less holiday.

Is there right and wrong in this? My rule of thumb has always been that, regardless of contractual hours, I will stick around to get the job done and if that means staying late, I stay late (or start early, as I'm better at the front end of the day). But I have a family and other interests and I have been pretty good at getting away so I can have supper at home at a reasonable time.

It is tempting to get on a high horse over this, either scorning those 'manacled to their desks' (no-one's last words on their death bed have ever been: *"I wish I'd spent more time in the office"*); or berating those who will never climb the ladder of success (*"if you can't take the heat, get out of the kitchen"*).

In his stimulating book 'Thank God it's Monday', Mark Greene asserts there is no one size fits all 'correct' approach; rather, our working day will depend on our goals, stage in life and capability. If we work out a balance in our own lives between these, we won't go far wrong.

I believe this is really important - not just a nicety, or a matter of personal preference. For without breaks and proper rest, we are likely to grow stale and unhealthy. Creativity ebbs as stress levels rise, and our relationships can suffer. To allow others to work less hours, even if we choose to work longer, demonstrates respect for different lifestyles, and therefore each other.

CREATIVITY EBBS AS STRESS LEVELS RISE

Research by the Boston Consulting Group for the Council of Fashion Designers of America, observed that:
"in recent years, evolutions in technology, consumer behaviours, weather and the retail cycle have challenged the role and impact of the current fashion system (of fashion shows ahead of the season)"

One of the key challenges to the current system covered this very issue: *"The danger of designer creative burnout: the confusion of the fashion cycle, coupled with the increased importance and complexity of pre-collections, leaves less time for the creative process and artisanship, and puts immense pressure on critical design and creative talent. Our interviewees expressed a desire for a future system that creates more structural, predictable downtime for design and creative talent."*

One specific challenge for me concerns Sundays. God set an example by working six days in creating the world, and then resting. The fourth Commandment picks up this pattern: *"Remember the Sabbath day by keeping it holy. Six days you shall labour and do all your work, but the seventh day is a sabbath to the Lord your God. On it you shall not do any work, neither you, nor your son or daughter, nor your male or female servant, nor your animals, nor any foreigner residing in your towns."*

Do the complexities of 21st Century life mean it is simply not possible to keep this 'rule' - not least because, in a multi cultural society, different religious groups have different days of observance?

I would suggest that the principal remains, but it needs to be applied flexibly.

For myself, I have worked four Sundays each year for most of my working life, as these have been in the middle of London Fashion Week, the focus of my daily work.

To have been absent on these days would not have been understood by my work colleagues and would, in my view, have put in question the relevance to everyday life of the God that I was off worshipping. (For the record, the team always have days off in lieu to cover these Sundays worked.)

Other Sundays, though, I have kept special, trying to avoid everyday work.

LET'S HAVE A REST FROM THE IDEA THAT THERE'S SOMETHING MORALLY SUPERIOR ABOUT OVERWORK, AND THAT THE HIGHEST HUMAN CALLING IS TO BE A PERFECT COG IN A CAPITALIST MACHINE. LET'S CELEBRATE HOLIDAYS AS A WELL-EARNED ACHIEVEMENT. IF ASPIRATION MEANS ANYTHING, IT SHOULD BE THE DESIRE NOT JUST FOR A GOOD JOB, BUT FOR A GOOD LIFE
Helen Lewis, journalist

THE QUESTION FOR MANY PEOPLE IS ABOUT WHETHER THEIR OVERALL LIFE GIVES THEM OPPORTUNITIES TO FLOURISH AS HUMAN BEINGS. THIS INVOLVES BOTH FULFILLING DUTIES AND HAVING THE OPPORTUNITY TO BE A GOOD STEWARD OF WHAT GOD HAS ENTRUSTED TO US
Mark Greene

19 ORIGINAL OR COPY?

... TEN TIPS TO HELP NAVIGATE THE MINEFIELD OF INTELLECTUAL PROPERTY

ANY industry with creativity at its heart is always going to have challenges around what is the original and what is a copy. The worlds of art and antiques are particularly well known for this, with many a TV programme seeking to lift the veil - often with considerable amounts of cash at stake.

Fashion also has its fair share of imitation, and sorting out what is original, what is a copy, and how to prove it, is something of a minefield.

Gary Assim has specialised in fashion intellectual property for many years and shares his experience on how to decide who owns what.

IF you want to be distinctive, if you want to be known, and if you want to make money, you need to understand 'what is intellectual property?' and the boundaries between inspiration and copying!

For most fashion designers, intellectual property commonly arises as a trade mark, like the name of the designer or the brand, or a design right, like the shape, pattern or combination of features of an item. Both are important to protect, otherwise you might end up losing the right to use your own name, because someone else owns the trade mark to it, or you let others copy your designs at will because you were unaware you could stop them and did not register your rights!

Here are ten tips to avoid the worst pitfalls ...

GARY ASSIM *heads up legal firm Shoosmith's national Retail and Intellectual Property & Creative Industry Groups, in which he has built up strong reputations, on both a national and international basis. He specialises in the clothing and footwear industry, acting for start-ups and global fashion brands, helping them understand the value of IP and advising on international growth strategies.*

1. WHEN you set up a business, e.g. Alex McKing Ltd, register your name (Alex McKing) as a trade mark *(see https://www.gov.uk/register-a-trademark)* - but so that YOU are the owner, not the limited company. This is important for when someone wants to invest or buy your business. They will ask your trade mark to be transferred to the company and this is the trigger for you to decide if the investment is enough to give up control of your name!

2. WHEN creating new designs, try and keep a mood board or electronic folder of your inspiration. This is helpful, first, if someone complains that you have copied their work. It allows a lawyer to check if this is correct or not, based on what's on your mood board/folder. Don't worry if the other person's design is on your mood board/folder, it does not automatically mean you have copied it! Secondly, if you complain about someone else copying your work, your lawyer can do the same check in reverse about their inspiration.

3. ALWAYS remember to date and initial your design drawings. It is useful evidence when trying to prove that you did actually create the design (and not an intern!) on the date you said.

4. DO not believe the old wives' tale that, if you make three, five, seven (or however many) changes to someone else's design, then you will not be copying. This is absolute rubbish. You could make 100 changes and still be guilty of copying, because you will have changed everything apart from the feature that attracted you to the design in the first place, which usually is the only feature in the whole design that is protected!

5. DO not enter into any contract without someone else looking at it. Especially, be wary of agency contracts that look as if they only last a year, but actually cannot be terminated for a further twelve months, and then only by paying compensation.

6. FROM my experience, the designers that have 'made it' have had great support from someone else, be it a school or university friend, family member or trusted advisor. It takes a great weight off designers knowing that someone else is looking after the business side of things. Don't try and do it all yourself – it's too hard!

7. DON'T believe everything you read about yourself, no matter how great it is, because PR does not pay the bills – selling your collection does.

8. REMEMBER, intellectual property is territorial in its protection. So, if you register your name in the UK only, as a trade mark it is not protected elsewhere - not even in Europe! You should consider which countries and regions are important to you (as it is very expensive to register a trade mark all over the world), and just register in those countries to start with. Whatever you do ensure you have the UK and China covered.

9. WHERE you are trying to be distinctive, remember that a combination of known features could be novel if they have never been combined before.

10. WHENEVER you can afford one, get a great lawyer to help you protect, develop and grow your fashion brand!!

I 10 A LOT OF GAY PEOPLE WORK IN FASHION

A THREAT TO BELIEF OR AN OPPORTUNITY TO LOVE?

THERE are a lot of gay people in fashion, many of whom I have thoroughly enjoyed working with over many years.

As a Christian, though, if I take seriously the traditional reading of the Bible, which I do, I find myself in a tricky corner here. For it seems pretty clear, from the early chapters of Genesis onwards, that gay relationships are not the model set out as the context for marriage.

Of course, this dilemma is not just mine; it is an issue that threatens to blow apart the unity of the world-wide church. And, with the UK's Marriage (Same Sex Couples) Act 2013, many outside faith communities are troubled at what they see as a fundamental change to the historic basis of marriage.

What to do? A couple of (I hope) obvious comments. Firstly, God loves everyone *(John 3:16),* and I will seek to do likewise. Secondly, all are given free will to make their own decisions and I, for one, have no intentions of interfering with that fundamental human freedom.

And then, I see absolutely no justification for any form of 'anti-gay' sentiment or rhetoric in today's multi-cultural society. To do so, even if one is taking a standpoint based on an honest reading of the Bible, is divisive, judgmental and uncaring.

I like a comment Pope Francis is alleged to have made: *A person once asked me, in a provocative manner, if I approved of homosexuality. I replied with another question: "Tell me, when God looks at a gay person, does He endorse the existence of this person with love, or reject and condemn this person?"* I assume that the Pope's unspoken reply is that God endorses them with love.

THIS HAS BEEN THE MOST DIFFICULT SECTION OF THE BOOK TO WRITE

THOSE reading this, but not sharing my faith, may raise an eyebrow, saying that no one else has a problem here - the church needs to "keep up with the times" and get relevant.

I don't think it is as simple as that, though, either for Christians or those of the other Abrahamic monotheistic faiths, Judaism and Islam. There is no integrity in abandoning, just because culture changes, what has been handed down over centuries as foundational truth.

As I see it, and this is certainly not an official church position, God is big enough to deal with what we see as an insoluble problem. That people have gone their own way and not kept Him centre stage must pain God's heart. And this plays out across all behavioural patterns, not just sexuality. Yet, over the millenia, a holy God has demonstrated that He is patient and gracious.

My belief is that God is most interested in people loving one another - Jesus stated that quite clearly. And He would want us, whether Christians or not, to take that as our starting point. From there, we can discuss this matter, with gentleness and humility, even if there is no immediate 'answer'.

Over the years, in the face of so much blind bigotry and mocking dismissiveness, many in the gay community have chosen to take a militant line over what they see as their right to choose their partners and pattern of relationship. My hope is that those on both sides of this dilemma can take an open-minded approach and accept that it is not immediately resolvable. It is an opportunity to love, rather than a threat to belief.

This has been the most difficult section of the book to write - and not just as I am trying to reconcile very different positions. It is because pondering it leads me into the very heart of God. And there, I often find things that are beyond my comprehension.

But, that is a place where we can find out amazing things about ourselves, each other, and the world we live in. It is a work in progress.

... finally ... a little bit of
KINDNESS *goes a long way*

A PERSONAL REFLECTION ON FASHION'S REPUTATION

RESEARCH carried out among young people concerning careers in fashion, revealed that many thought the industry was a brutal place and not very nice to work in - even though they would love to get into it.

This is understandable, as the intense pressure of the fashion cycle takes no prisoners, and it is a very competitive business. Add to this that fashion attracts some very pushy people, and it is easy to see how it has acquired such a reputation.

I'm not going to argue with this, but I will observe, after thirty-five years working in fashion, that it is also a vibrant place to be, with many talented and inspiring people, giving 100+%.

I've been particularly thankful for a succession of great people making up the team at the British Fashion Council.

Yet, I have a plea and a prayer for those working in fashion; it is this: take a little more time and space to be kind. It doesn't cost anything, and can be quite transformational.

I believe kindness, and its close relative compassion, sit at the centre of God's heart for fashion.

I HAVE A PLEA AND A PRAYER: TAKE A LITTLE MORE TIME AND SPACE TO BE KIND. IT DOESN'T COST ANYTHING AND CAN BE QUITE TRANSFORMATIONAL

KINDNESS IS ALWAYS
FASHIONABLE AND
ALWAYS WELCOME
Amelia Barr - novelist

FOR BEAUTIFUL EYES, LOOK
FOR THE GOOD IN OTHERS;
FOR BEAUTIFUL LIPS, SPEAK
ONLY WORDS OF KINDNESS
Audrey Hepburn - actress

NO ACT OF KINDNESS
NO MATTER HOW SMALL
IS EVER WASTED
Aesop - philosopher

AS GOD'S CHOSEN PEOPLE
HOLY AND DEARLY LOVED
CLOTHE YOURSELVES WITH
COMPASSION, KINDNESS,
HUMILITY, GENTLENESS
AND PATIENCE
St Paul - Colossians 3:12

YOU EITHER BELIEVE THAT
PEOPLE RESPOND TO
AUTHORITY, OR THAT THEY
RESPOND TO KINDNESS.
I'M IN THE LATTER CAMP
Brian Eno - musician

THIS FASHION BUSINESS
IS A BIT LIKE ONE BIG
DYSFUNCTIONAL FAMILY
Overheard!

THE SOLDIER'S FRIEND

KINDNESS IN ACTION

EMMA WILLIS MBE

EMMA started her Jermyn Street bespoke shirt label in 1987, moving her all-English production to a Gloucester town house in 2010.

In 2007, Emma founded a charity, *Style for Soldiers,* to support servicemen recovering at the Headley Court rehabilitation centre in Surrey.

Emma was awarded an MBE in 2014.

THANK YOU FOR THE
WONDERFUL GIFTS
YOU HAVE GIVEN ME;
FOR HELPING ME TO FEEL
SMART AND COMFORTABLE
WHEN I WAS BROKEN - *Tom*

BACK TO THE BEGINNING?

IT was in 2007, driving along listening to a Radio 4 programme from Headley Court Military Rehabilitation Centre. I was so moved, I cried as I sat at the wheel: one man had lost his vision, another his legs.

So terrible - they were courageous about their injuries, but their biggest fear was having to leave the Forces: it was their career, their identity, their confidence, their friendships, their family. A lot of them had joined up very young, and it had filled up their lives with purpose and meaning.

I wanted to do something. I'd worked with disabled people at Fulham and Hammersmith MENCAP, so I should be OK working with disability.

I knew I had to contact someone at Headley Court. It took me about a year to get in. Quite rightly there was huge security - they have to make sure you're doing it for the right reasons.

Although I wanted to do more, I started by going in at Christmas and simply gave a present of a shirt.

My business backer, Bill Tyne, when he started to support me in 2000, had said that he wanted me to affiliate the Emma Willis company with a charity. And I was absolutely in agreement. He used to send me brochures with suggestions for charities to support.

So, when the idea for Style for Soldiers came about, Bill was right behind me.

THEY WERE COURAGEOUS ABOUT THEIR INJURIES,
BUT THEIR BIGGEST FEAR WAS HAVING TO LEAVE THE FORCES:
IT WAS THEIR CAREER, THEIR IDENTITY, THEIR CONFIDENCE,
THEIR FRIENDSHIPS, THEIR FAMILY

WALKING STICKS

THE soldiers I started to meet had NHS walking sticks which, understandably, they were not too keen on.

I designed one made of black ebony wood with a buffalo horn handle. This enabled me to create a proper orthopaedic grip. And I included a silver band with their name and regiment on.

So the sticks appeared more of a fashion accessory than a medical aid.

CHRISTMAS PARTY

BY 2011, many of the former patients were starting to be discharged from Headley Court. I started an annual reunion, the Christmas party. This brings together injured servicemen and their families, with empathetic people from the business world, who buy tickets so the soldiers can attend free. Everybody mingles, no one is on their own. It works so well, helping the soldiers' confidence. It's a path into the civilian world.

PARTNERS

ONE of the great things has been how many people have come on board to help. At first it was me, shirts and sticks. But I wanted to give the soldiers more.

Firstly, James Lock & Co helped out with hats. Then I moved on to suits. They would be crucial as the soldiers moved to civilian life. It couldn't be Savile Row, as there were 600 soldiers on my database, and it would have been far too expensive.

I tried to get into M&S, as I was buying suits online for collection around the country. M&S loved the idea. I had a look at the cost of basic suits and asked for 200 vouchers at £250. They gave 250 vouchers for £400, which meant the soldiers could go for the best suit! As I left the meeting, they said that, when I got to the end of the 250 vouchers, "don't run out, ask, and we'll give you 250 more".

M&S have been wonderful, offering style advice as well as the vouchers. They never use the wonderful feedback from the soldiers to gain press coverage: it is passed straight back to the staff who have helped.

The manners of the servicemen are amazing: they take nothing for granted and are so appreciative. They appreciate beautiful clothes as much as anyone I've met.

BUILDING SUPPORT

I tried to build up a wide range of collaborations, including with hotels for the soldiers to stay in when attending the reunions, and restaurants for meetings. Mappin & Webb provide watches and cuff links. These are really important for a triple amputee. They deserve something beautiful on their prosthetic arm.

Mappin & Webb were launching a campaign watch, based on the WW1 watch they gave to soldiers in the trenches. They relaunched it to tie in with the centenary and agreed to give a percentage of proceeds to Style for Soldiers and donate five watches. And they agreed to design a commemorative cuff link to commemorate the two operations in Afghanistan and Iraq. We liaised with our General, who gave us the exact colours and stripes, and what they meant. They made 100 cufflinks and gave us fifty for soldiers.

David Gandy and Ryan Palmer's London Sock Company have given 100s of socks and raised £3,000 at a silent auction from stuffed socks sewn together with monkeys faces and hugged by David in a café on Instagram! This will pay for a young injured serviceman's honeymoon.

I have held one reunion each year and one fundraiser. For one of these, the headmaster of Eton sent along the college's music scholars to perform at the Ritz - phenomenal.

Mr Porter has been a major sponsor and supporter since day one. Conde Nast have given free adverts, Crown Estates pay for the hire of Spencer House for parties. Smith Williamson and Church House are helping with financial advice. The soldiers have to live off their compensation money for the rest of their lives. Wives and partners have to give up work: its particularly difficult for them especially if they have children.

photo: Ben Weller. The Mr Porter fashion shoot for Style for Soldiers

PATRONAGE

DAILY Telegraph fashion editor, Lisa Armstrong came on board as a Patron immediately I asked her, as did male model David Gandy. They got on like a house on fire with the military, initially General Sir Richard Shirreff. There seemed to be so much overlap between the military and fashion worlds.

This was crucial, as I had the military credibility and the fashion credibility needed to build the work.

The Conde Nast support gave real glamour and my dream, in due course, is to secure Royal patronage.

A BRIDGE BETWEEN THE NEED OF THE SOLDIERS AND THE KINDNESS OF MY CUSTOMERS

A BRIDGE

I also raise money to run things through my customers. I send them a regular newsletter and always tell the story of one of the soldiers. This creates a bridge between the need of the soldiers and the kindness of my customers.

MONEY LAUNDERING!

AT the 2015 Christmas party, a huge cheer went up as I read out a letter from the Chancellor of the Exchequer, apologising for not being able to attend, but awarding £1.5million to Style for Soldiers - from the recent banking fines.

In the words of our Patron, Major General Sir George Norton, this was "a very happy bit of modern day money laundering!"

CAPTAIN STUART CROXFORD suffered severe injuries to his feet when his vehicle hit a mine in Afghanistan in 2012. Capt. Croxford, from Portsmouth, then lost his lower right leg in 2014, as a result of a sailing accident while he was taking part in a rehabilitation initiative.

"When I was at Headley Court, I heard there was a lady who gave away shirts and walking sticks, so I joined the queue. But the shirt is only the start. She spends so much time getting to know each soldier, keeping in touch with them, arranging opportunities and mentoring for them. It was because of encouragement from her, that I have set up a powerboat racing team for ex-servicemen. I was lucky enough to be given a bespoke Huntsman suit. I have just left the Army, and now I'm in the process of speaking to potential employers, wearing the clothes I got through Style For Soldiers. It massively boosts your self-confidence."

NOW I'M IN THE PROCESS OF SPEAKING TO POTENTIAL EMPLOYERS, WEARING THE CLOTHES I GOT THROUGH STYLE FOR SOLDIERS. IT MASSIVELY BOOSTS YOUR SELF CONFIDENCE

SAPPER HENRY SAKYI, from Stoke-on-Trent, suffered from frostbite during a training exercise in Poland in 2011 that permanently damaged the nerves in his hands and feet, and later contracted throat cancer. He lost half his body weight during chemotherapy and went to Headley Court to learn how to walk and speak again.

"After I took part in a photo shoot for Style For Soldiers, I told Emma that I loved the clothes and the way they made me feel more than any money or anything else she could have given me. It made me feel I could achieve anything I wanted, and it has helped me to go from being homeless to having a job, a mortgage and my own home."

I LOVED THE CLOTHES AND THE WAY THEY MADE ME FEEL - MORE THAN ANY MONEY OR ANYTHING ELSE SHE COULD HAVE GIVEN ME. IT MADE ME FEEL I COULD ACHIEVE ANYTHING I WANTED

*Stories courtesy of Gordon Rayner
Chief Reporter, Daily Telegraph
19th December 2015 www.telegraph.co.uk*

IS STYLE FOR SOLDIERS JUST A GOOD WORK?

I didn't realise it would be so important for the Emma Willis business. The partnerships I've developed through Style for Soldiers have given me and my brand such credibility - to have the faith and support of people who wouldn't otherwise have been able to get involved with a commercial venture. Its been an incredibly positive thing.

Sometimes it seems too much, and people have asked whether I'm jeopardising my business, my family life and, yes, sometimes it seems a bit much. I have taken someone on to help, but it's so personal ... personal connections.

There is no doubt, though, that what you put into life you get back with interest.

THE FUTURE?

THE reunion parties are such an important thing. Many of us look forward to a summer holiday, but to give the soldiers something they can look forward to is really important. And it has to be long term, as some of the soldiers have long term rehabilitation - one has had no less than forty operations - and post traumatic stress can set in up to ten years afterwards. I'd love not just to increase the number of parties around the country, but also to make them a place to dress up for, maybe using industry experts to help style the soldiers and their wives. And I know they would help - the industry has thrown up such angels!

A FINAL WORD

I'VE never seen such human kindness as at Headley Court. The staff go way beyond just doing their job. The soldiers are always looking out for someone more injured than themselves.

THE PARTNERSHIPS I'VE DEVELOPED THROUGH STYLE FOR SOLDIERS HAVE GIVEN ME AND MY BRAND SUCH CREDIBILITY

Ambassador, David Gandy with Sock Monkeys

THE INDUSTRY HAS THROWN UP SUCH ANGELS!

I'VE NEVER SEEN SUCH HUMAN KINDNESS AS AT HEADLEY COURT

REFLECTIONS ON WHAT GOD
MIGHT HAVE TO SAY TO THE
FASHION INDUSTRY IN THE
PRESENT DAY ... AND WHAT
IT MIGHT ASK OF HIM

GOD'S HEART

6

TEN PERSPECTIVES ON GOD'S HEART FOR FASHION

if God was in charge of fashion
... how would He run it?

1 CALLED TO BE COUNTER CULTURAL

FRUITFUL LIVES BRINGING JESUS
INTO THE WORLD OF FASHION

THE world of fashion is a driven place to work in. I know - I was there for a long time! It is very full on, and takes few prisoners. A colleague working in a related industry once confided, "Simon, there are easier ways to earn a living!"

Those following in the footsteps of Jesus, though, will march to a different beat.

The fruit of the Spirit, set out by Paul in his letter to the Galatians, gives sound principles and, in the pages that follow, I suggest some further perspectives on what God's heart for fashion, and those working in it, might look like.

GOD'S PEOPLE ARE CALLED TO BE COUNTER-CULTURAL

WHAT happens when we live God's way? He brings gifts into our lives, much the same way that fruit appears in an orchard - things like affection for others, exuberance about life, serenity. We develop a willingness to stick with things, a sense of compassion in the heart, and a conviction that basic holiness permeates things and people. We find ourselves involved in loyal commitments, not needing to force our way in life, able to marshal and direct our energies wisely.

Galatians 5:22,23 The Message

LOVE

JOY

PEACE

PATIENCE

KINDNESS

GOODNESS

FAITHFULNESS

GENTLENESS

SELF CONTROL

WHAT HAPPENS WHEN
WE LIVE GOD'S WAY?

#2

TEN BEATITUDES
FOR FASHION

IF JESUS WAS MY MENTOR WHAT CHARACTERISTICS
WOULD HE LOOK TO DEVELOP IN ME?

BLESSED are those who give the glory to God for their gifts, for only they will realise the fullness of what they have been given

BLESSED are those who share any sense of inadequacy, for they will find great encouragement from friends around them

BLESSED are those who avoid seeking the praise of others, for God will reveal his appreciation in ways undreamed of

BLESSED are those who work to see fair treatment for all those earning their livelihood in fashion, for their longing will be fulfilled

BLESSED are those who avoid criticising others harshly, for they will be shown great kindness

BLESSED are the pure in heart, for they will see God Himself bringing their work to life

BLESSED are the peacemakers, for they will create an environment where all are able to flourish

BLESSED are those who are sidelined because of their beliefs, for God will raise them up to carry out his purposes

BLESSED are you when people scorn you for your faith. Don't just grin and bear it; smile, as you are standing in line with a countless army down the centuries

BLESSED are those who allow their distinctive saltiness to challenge unhealthy behaviours and shine the light they have received to reveal exploitation and injustice

beatitude, *n.* blessedness

blessed, *adj.* consecrated;
revered; fortunate

The Concise Oxford Dictionary

based on Matthew 5:3-16

BLESSED ARE THOSE WHO AVOID SEEKING THE PRAISE OF OTHERS FOR GOD WILL REVEAL HIS APPRECIATION IN WAYS UNDREAMED OF

LET JUSTICE ROLL LIKE A RIVER
RIGHTEOUSNESS LIKE A NEVER FAILING STREAM
Amos 5:24

3 PLEA FOR HELP

CRYING OUT FROM A TESTING WORKPLACE

GOD, MY GOD, I AM IN DISTRESS
AND UNABLE TO LIFT MYSELF
FROM THE HOLE I SEEM TO BE IN

I am weighed down with work, deadlines looming, inspiration needed, pressure bearing down from those around me and, most of all, from my own demanding self. I worry that I am unequal to the task, that whispering voices look on and witness how I am struggling.

I cry out to You, yet an unseen voice countermands my words, telling me to knuckle down and get the job done. I lie awake at night, my mind arguing things through, real and imagined. I am wearied by it all. Can I go on?

I am tempted to despair, to self pity ... but then a verse drops into my head:

No test that comes your way is beyond the course of what others have had to face. All you need to remember is that God will never let you down. He'll never yet you be pushed past your limit; He'll always be there to help you come through it. (1 Cor 10:13)

I run to Your Word and see that many before me have been just here, right where I am now. I share with friends, and they too recognise the place I am in.

God, my God, You know me, have done since before I was born. You never said that life with You would be easy, but that You would be there for me. You are, and I thank You and praise You, for You are a great God, who displays Your love and power each day in Your people's lives.

Amen

I CRIED OUT TO GOD
FOR HELP; I CRIED OUT
TO GOD TO HEAR ME
WHEN I WAS IN DISTRESS;
I SOUGHT THE LORD AT
NIGHT; I STRETCHED
OUT UNTIRING HANDS
AND MY SOUL REFUSED
TO BE COMFORTED
Psalm 77:1,2

I WILL MEDITATE ON
ALL YOUR WORKS AND
CONSIDER ALL YOUR
MIGHTY DEEDS
Psalm 77:12

YOU ARE THE GOD
WHO PERFORMS
MIRACLES; YOU DISPLAY
YOUR POWER AMONGST
THE PEOPLES; WITH
YOUR MIGHTY ARM YOU
REDEEMED YOUR PEOPLE
Psalm 77:14,15

prayer based on Psalm 77

#4   A LETTER TO BELIEVERS

"THESE ARE THE WORDS OF HIM WHO IS
THE AUTHOR OF CREATIVITY"

TO MY BELOVED CHILDREN
working in the world of fashion:

These are the words of Him who is the author of creativity, who planned out the seasons, clothed Adam and Eve, longs for justice, died that you might live ... who is the same yesterday and today and forever.

I know all about you - your creativity, your hard work, your passion, and I love these. I also know that you long for me to be with you every step of the way, empowering you on your journey. This I applaud. Keep on, for these are key to living life well.

Yet, I would alert you to two things, for these are on my heart in this day. Do not just look inwards, to each other for support and encouragement. Share the message of power and hope that flow from the Cross with all those around you, asking me to show you how to set about it. For I know that so many seem so indifferent but, trust me, there are many that will respond to my love, if they see it at work in you.

And then, though the world will remain a broken place, with much suffering, until I return, I want you to pour yourselves into transforming the way things are done, where you have influence. It will not be easy, but no lasting change to structures and the way things are done will be achieved without my power being released through prayer, as I dwell powerfully in you day by day. Only then will you have the joy of seeing lasting change.

Now, I offer you myself:
CHRIST IN YOU, THE HOPE OF GLORY.

STRUGGLING WITH ALL HIS ENERGY WHICH, SO POWERFULLY, WORKS IN ME
Colossians 1:29

THERE ARE MANY THAT WILL RESPOND TO MY LOVE IF THEY SEE IT AT WORK IN YOU

I OFFER YOU MYSELF:
CHRIST IN YOU
THE HOPE OF GLORY

letter based on Revelation 2 & 3 with a sprinkling of Colossians 1:24-29

#5 LOVE SONG FOR FASHION

I LOVE YOUR CREATIVITY
... *it echoes my overflowing heart*

I LOVE YOUR PASSION
... *it takes life and lives it to the full*

I LOVE YOUR INDUSTRIOUSNESS
... *it achieves great things*

I LOVE YOUR PRIDE
... *it shows commitment to what you do*

I LOVE YOUR
PASSION

I LONG FOR YOU TO LOVE ME BACK
... *as I love you*

I LONG FOR YOUR PASSION
... *to focus itself on Me*

I LONG FOR YOUR WORK
... *not to become an end in itself*

I LONG FOR YOUR ACHIEVEMENT
... *to give glory to the Creator of creatives*

I LONG FOR YOU
TO LOVE ME BACK
AS I LOVE YOU

WILL YOU RISK
... *joining your love to Mine?*

WILL YOU OPEN YOURSELF
... *into My loving arms?*

WILL YOU TAKE TIME OUT
... *to spend time with Me?*

WILL YOU BE CONTENT WITH SECOND
... *and place Me at the centre?*

WILL YOU RISK
JOINING YOUR
LOVE TO MINE?

LET HIS BANNER OVER ME BE LOVE

6   A CAUTIONARY WORD

FASHION IS A DANGEROUS MASTER

IN their right context, clothes can be an entirely positive enhancement of who we are and how we are seen.

In the wrong context, they can deceive us into distorting our priorities, both in how we see ourselves and others.

Caution ... fashion is a good servant, but a dangerous master. It has the power to liberate or enslave ... SO HANDLE WITH CARE!

YOUR BEAUTY SHOULD NOT COME FROM OUTWARD ADORNMENT, SUCH AS ELABORATE HAIRSTYLES AND THE WEARING OF GOLD JEWELLERY OR FINE CLOTHES. RATHER, IT SHOULD BE THAT OF YOUR INNER SELF, THE UNFADING BEAUTY OF A GENTLE AND QUIET SPIRIT, WHICH IS OF GREAT WORTH IN GOD'S SIGHT *1 Peter 3:3,4*

SUPPOSE A MAN COMES INTO YOUR MEETING WEARING A GOLD RING AND FINE CLOTHES, AND A POOR MAN IN FILTHY OLD CLOTHES ALSO COMES IN. IF YOU SHOW SPECIAL ATTENTION TO THE MAN WEARING FINE CLOTHES AND SAY, "HERE'S A GOOD SEAT FOR YOU," BUT SAY TO THE POOR MAN, "YOU STAND THERE" OR "SIT ON THE FLOOR BY MY FEET," HAVE YOU NOT DISCRIMINATED AMONG YOURSELVES AND BECOME JUDGES WITH EVIL THOUGHTS? *James 2:2-4*

FASHION HAS THE POWER TO LIBERATE OR ENSLAVE

HANDLE WITH CARE!

DO NOT WORRY ABOUT YOUR LIFE, WHAT YOU WILL EAT OR DRINK; OR ABOUT YOUR BODY, WHAT YOU WILL WEAR. IS NOT LIFE MORE THAN FOOD, AND THE BODY MORE THAN CLOTHES? BUT SEEK FIRST HIS KINGDOM AND HIS RIGHTEOUSNESS, AND ALL THESE THINGS WILL BE GIVEN TO YOU AS WELL *Matthew 6:25,33*

7 A PRAYER

FOR COLLEAGUES WORKING IN FASHION

AT the heart of the Christian message lies an unavoidable crossroads, one that requires a decision and a leap of faith.

We can argue about what we call the Supreme Being, or whether there is one. We can wax lyrical about Jesus being a good man and an inspiring teacher. We can applaud the great things His church has achieved over the years ... or lament the far from great endeavours it has also pursued.

I hope that the stories and issues raised in this book are helpful examples and challenges to us all in our everyday lives, whether or not we are people of faith.

However, the time comes where we must decide whether the God who has hovered over all that I have spoken of, is a distant, if benevolent, uncle figure, whom we respect, but do not expect to have a major influence on who we are, what we do, or how.

Or, if He is who He claims to be, the one and only Creator God who sent His Son, Jesus Christ, to die on a cross to restore us to the intended, intimate relationship with Him, and start the process of bringing transformational healing and restoration, not just to individual lives, but nations, economies and the very planet itself. For the clear teaching of the Bible He inspired to be written, is that we will be unable to achieve anything lasting by ourselves. *(Romans 3:23)*

To entertain, let alone accept this, is a big step. My prayer is that THE CHARACTER OF FASHION will help you, if you have not yet considered this ultimate question of life's meaning and purpose - including everyday life in the world of fashion and any other - to do so.

Below is a suggested prayer to bring before God. Be assured, He will respect your approach. And, similarly, if you choose not to, He will respect that too.

DEAR GOD

I WANT TO LIVE A LIFE THAT FULLY EMPLOYS MY ABILITIES.

I WANT TO MAKE A DIFFERENCE, TO THE WAY THE WORLD WORKS AND THE LIVES OF THOSE AROUND ME.

I WANT TO SEE THINGS DONE IN A JUST WAY, THAT RESPECTS INDIVIDUALS, BRINGS HOPE AND PRESERVES OUR PLANET.

PLEASE HELP ME TO CONSIDER HOW I CAN BEST ACHIEVE THESE GOALS ... AND WHERE YOU MIGHT FIT IN.

AMEN

#8 ARMOUR NEEDED

BE STRONG IN THE LORD AND IN HIS MIGHTY POWER

LIKE many workplaces fashion can, at times, be brutal and challenging. We can either take the view that this is life, and we have to battle our way through in our own strength ... or, and this is the biblical view, that there is no need to fear these times, if we take seriously, and put on, God's armour. For the fiercest battles are usually spiritual, and need to be approached accordingly.

This can then help us to look more kindly at those who seem to be a thorn in our side, as they may be having a hard time themselves and need to be cut some slack, not hit back at. Only this way can we break the descending spiral of unkindness that can all too easily follow. I defeat my enemies by making them my friends. Tricky, but entirely possible, if I am surrounded by the security of God's armour.

PUT ON THE FULL ARMOUR OF GOD
SO THAT, WHEN THE DAY OF EVIL
COMES, YOU MAY BE ABLE TO
STAND YOUR GROUND.

STAND FIRM THEN WITH THE BELT
OF TRUTH BUCKLED AROUND
YOUR WAIST, THE BREASTPLATE OF
RIGHTEOUSNESS IN PLACE, WITH
YOUR FEET FITTED WITH THE
READINESS THAT COMES FROM
THE GOSPEL OF PEACE.

IN ADDITION, TAKE UP THE SHIELD
OF FAITH, WITH WHICH YOU CAN
EXTINGUISH ALL THE FLAMING
ARROWS OF THE EVIL ONE.

TAKE THE HELMET OF SALVATION
AND THE SWORD OF THE SPIRIT
WHICH IS THE WORD OF GOD

AND PRAY IN THE SPIRIT ON ALL OCCASIONS
WITH ALL KINDS OF PRAYERS AND REQUESTS

Ephesians 6:13-18

BE STRONG IN THE LORD
AND IN HIS MIGHTY
POWER, FOR OUR
STRUGGLE IS NOT
AGAINST FLESH AND
BLOOD BUT AGAINST ...
THE SPIRITUAL FORCES
OF EVIL *Ephesians 6:10,12*

CONSIDER IT PURE JOY
WHENEVER YOU FACE
TRIALS OF MANY KINDS,
BECAUSE THE TESTING OF
YOUR FAITH PRODUCES
PERSEVERANCE
James 1:2,3

9 CLOTHES IN A HOLY PLACE

PUT ON CLEAN CLOTHES OF RIGHTEOUSNESS

image: Katrina Lawson Johnston

ISRAEL, O ISRAEL, WHY DID YOU TURN YOUR BACK
ON ME? I CHOSE YOU TO REPRESENT ME ON EARTH.
YOU HAD SUCH HUGE POTENTIAL FOR GOOD. YET
YOU WENT YOUR OWN WAY, AND IT ALL WENT
WRONG. YOUR EXILE WAS YOUR OWN DOING. BUT
NOW IT IS TIME TO RETURN ... JOSHUA, AS HIGH
PRIEST YOU REPRESENT MY PEOPLE. TAKE OFF THE
FILTHY CLOTHES YOU ARE WEARING, THEY REMIND
ME OF ISRAEL'S WAYWARDNESS. I HAVE FORGIVEN
YOU AND NOW GIVE YOU A FRESH START. PUT ON
CLEAN CLOTHES OF RIGHTEOUSNESS. THEY WILL
REMIND YOU OF HOW I WANT YOU TO LIVE

Author's adapted and expanded text based on Zechariah 3:3,4

THE SOLDIERS ... STRIPPED HIM AND PUT A SCARLET ROBE
ON HIM ... THEY KNELT BEFORE HIM AND MOCKED HIM.
... AFTER THEY HAD MOCKED HIM, THEY TOOK OFF THE
ROBE AND PUT HIS OWN CLOTHES ON HIM. THEN THEY
LED HIM OUT TO CRUCIFY HIM ... WHEN THEY CRUCIFIED
HIM, THEY DIVIDED UP HIS CLOTHES BY CASTING LOTS

Matthew 27:27-35

AS I LOOKED UP INTO HEAVEN ... I SAW SOMEONE LIKE
A SON OF MAN, DRESSED IN A ROBE REACHING DOWN TO
HIS FEET AND WITH A GOLDEN SASH AROUND HIS CHEST ...
HIS FACE WAS LIKE THE SUN SHINING IN ALL ITS BRILLIANCE
... I FELL AT HIS FEET ... HE SAID: "DO NOT BE AFRAID,
I AM THE FIRST AND THE LAST. I AM THE LIVING ONE;
I WAS DEAD, AND BEHOLD I AM ALIVE FOR EVER AND EVER

Revelation 1:13-18

#10 GOD'S WARDROBE

WE LOVE BECAUSE GOD FIRST LOVED US
1 John 5:6

image: Katrina Lawson Johnston

CHOSEN BY GOD FOR
THIS NEW LIFE OF LOVE,
DRESS IN THE WARDROBE
GOD PICKED OUT FOR YOU:

COMPASSION
KINDNESS
HUMILITY

QUIET STRENGTH
DISCIPLINE

BE EVEN TEMPERED, CONTENT
WITH SECOND PLACE, QUICK TO
FORGIVE AN OFFENCE ... FORGIVE
AS QUICKLY AND COMPLETELY
AS THE MASTER FORGAVE YOU

AND, REGARDLESS OF
WHAT ELSE YOU PUT ON:

WEAR LOVE

IT'S YOUR BASIC
ALL-PURPOSE GARMENT
... NEVER BE WITHOUT IT

Let the peace of Christ keep you in tune
with each other, in step with each other.
None of this going off and doing your
own thing. And cultivate thankfulness.
Let the word of Christ have the run of
the house. Give it plenty of room in your
lives. Instruct and direct one another using
good common sense. *Colossians 3:12-16*

from THE MESSAGE: New Testament
© 1993 Eugene Peterson

A SHORT FASHION BIBLE STUDY

THERE'S an intriguing little passage
in Paul's letter to the Galatians: *You
are all children of God through faith
in Christ Jesus, for all of you who
were baptised into Christ have clothed
yourselves with Christ. Galatians 3:26,27*

Paul follows this by painting a picture
of heirs as children - they are like slaves,
even though they own the estate.

Similarly, God's people, prior to the
coming of Christ, had not received full
rights - they were struggling to keep
the Law, and failing ... miserably and
repeatedly. It was only when God sent
His Son, and then the Holy Spirit, that
the full rights as children of God were
released to and in them.

Just as heirs are free to enjoy the
benefits of the estate once they come of
age, so, with the grace of Christ and the
coming of the Holy Spirit, Christians
are empowered and free to enjoy the
benefits of Christ at work in them.

Back to the passage above - having
received Christ in baptism, we have
clothed ourselves with Christ. What
does this mean?

It means that we have a new status - we
are in Christ - but also that we are urged
to put on the wardrobe God has picked
out for us - *see the Colossians passage
alongside.* The subtlety I see is this: just
as the Spirit empowers our new life in
Christ, clothes can similarly take on a
whole new, fuller meaning: they can
not only express our personality; they
also act as a living picture of our
character as children of God.

WHAT DOES THE LORD
REQUIRE OF YOU?
TO ACT JUSTLY,
LOVE MERCY AND
WALK HUMBLY WITH
YOUR GOD *Micah 6:8*

7

TEN COMMANDMENTS
FOR FASHION

the heart of the matter

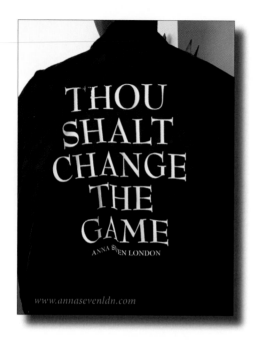

THOU SHALT CHANGE THE GAME

ANNA SEVEN LONDON

www.annasevenldn.com

FAIR PAY

EQUAL OPPORTUNITY

FOCUS ON YOUNG PEOPLE

ETHICAL AS THE NORM

KINDNESS IS KING

RESPONSIBILITY RULES

ENVIRONMENTAL PRIORITY

BENEFIT FOR ALL

LIFE WORK BALANCE

FORCE FOR GOOD

THE idea for a project called MULTI TALENTED GOD landed in February 2012, as I jotted down, over a cup of coffee one Saturday morning, what I thought might be God's priorities if He was in charge of fashion ... and what, therefore, we should all be praying for.

It turned out, entirely by "chance", to be a list of ten which, after the whirrings of my mischievous mind, became "God's 10 Commandments for Fashion."

Here, unamended, are my original ten. Of course, this does not pretend to be a definitive 'ten'. What do you think would be God's priorities for the world of fashion?

And what about where you work?

DON'T SHUFFLE ALONG, EYES TO THE GROUND, ABSORBED WITH THE THINGS IN FRONT OF YOU. LOOK UP AND BE ALERT TO WHAT IS GOING ON AROUND CHRIST - THAT'S WHERE THE ACTION IS. SEE THINGS FROM HIS PERSPECTIVE
Colossians 3:1,2 (The Message)

10

ALL those working in the industry
to be paid fairly for their work

OPPORTUNITIES to work in fashion
to be extended to all those with the ability
and desire, regardless of background

PARTICULAR emphasis to be placed
on access for school leavers and young
people with the introduction of a new
framework of apprenticeships and
other support schemes

ETHICALLY sound sources of
production, whether in the UK
or globally, to become the norm

ATTITUDES within the industry
to be given a complete overhaul,
with the elimination of all snobbery,
backbiting and unkindness

IMMEDIATE attention to be paid to
the effect of the industry on the wider
community including attitudes to
'beauty' and body shape and their
impact on young people

GLOBAL recycling schemes to be
explored to ensure unused clothing
is easily and quickly moved to areas
of need around the world - without
damaging local supply chains

SOCIAL ownership schemes, where
employees have a say in the business for
which they work, to become widespread

SUNDAY trading laws to be reviewed

FASHION to become a leading
global force for the good of all
in the 21st Century

A GREATEST COMMANDMENT
FOR FASHION?

MARK GREENE

MARK GREENE spent ten years working in advertising in London and New York and is prepared to admit it. After that, he studied at the London School of Theology, lectured in communications and served as Vice Principal before joining the London Institute for Contemporary Christianity as Executive Director. His many books include *Thank God it's Monday* and *Fruitfulness on the Frontline*.

WHEN JESUS WAS ASKED WHICH WAS THE GREATEST OF THE COMMANDMENTS, HE REPLIED: "LOVE THE LORD YOUR GOD WITH ALL YOUR HEART AND WITH ALL YOUR SOUL AND WITH ALL YOUR STRENGTH ... AND THE SECOND IS LIKE IT: "LOVE YOUR NEIGHBOUR AS YOURSELF." HE ADDED: "ALL THE LAW AND THE PROPHETS HANG ON THESE TWO COMMANDMENTS." *Matthew 22:37-40*

IF Jesus was asked which would be the *greatest* commandment for fashion, what I wonder would He reply?

Probably in exactly the same way, because His whole approach to life is, as He says, summarised in those two commandments. But what might it mean?

You love your neighbour in fashion by making clothes of beauty and integrity that do what particular types of clothes are meant to do – swirl at a dance, protect on a building site, express personality, celebrate the wonder and beauty of what it means to be human in body, mind, heart and spirit, communicate a role in a way that still honours the wearer (whether street cleaner or admiral) as a person created wondrously in the image of God ...

You love your neighbour in fashion by crafting things that expand people's understanding of beauty and style, rather than narrow it down: that serve to facilitate relationships, rather than setting up false barriers or imprisoning people in identikit group identities ...

You love your neighbour in fashion by not deliberately setting trends in clothes that sexualise children, privilege a very narrow range of body types or ages, turn men or women into objects ... or deliberately seek to inflame desire in others that the wearer has no goodly way of satisfying,

You love your neighbour in fashion by making sure that the people who manufacture cloth, cut, sew, label, pack, transport garments are paid a wage that allows them to put clothes on their children's backs, shoes on their feet, food in their stomachs, books in their hands and music in their ears ...

image: Katrina Lawson Johnston

YOU LOVE YOUR **NEIGHBOUR** IN FASHION
BY DRESSING TO EXPRESS ... NOT JUST IMPRESS

YOU love your neighbour in fashion by dressing to express not just impress, by dressing in ways that do not make other people feel small, that recognise that we live and work and play with other people in community and that to love others means to do all we can to build quality relationships with them, wanting the best for them ...

You love God in fashion by recognising that He is the great Creator, that every gift we have is from Him and is to be cherished and nurtured and enjoyed with care and humility for the sake of others...

And you love Him by remembering that He's your Father and that He delights to see you making the most of the gifts He's given you, delights to see you becoming more and more the person He created you to be ...

You love God in fashion by respecting the good world He created, the animals He gave life to, the land, trees, flowers He brought into being ... the wondrous velvet of a magnolia blossom, the sheening azure of an Aegean sky, the breathtaking elegance of a gazelle in motion.

You love God in fashion by wanting what you design, manufacture, market to please Him ... and asking for His help and inspiration in all you do ...

And you love God in fashion by putting Him before fashion ... by rejoicing that your identity is not found in the label you wear or own or sell, the collection you designed, the magazine you featured in, the title of your job ... but that your identity is to be found in relationship with the Father who loves you, the Son who gave His life for you, and the Spirit who empowers you to be the glorious true YOU that only He can help you be.

YOU LOVE **GOD** *IN* FASHION
BY PUTTING HIM *BEFORE* FASHION

THERE ARE RISKS AND COSTS TO
ACTION - BUT THEY ARE FAR LESS
THAN THE LONG RANGE RISKS
OF COMFORTABLE INACTION
John F Kennedy   35th US President

PUTTING PRINCIPLES
INTO ACTION

8

TEN FASHION CHALLENGES

turning talk into walk
... some suggestions

c1   WHO MADE MY CLOTHES?

EXPLOITATION or FAIR TRADE?

- **ISSUES?**   Where were my clothes made?
                  Are the workers who made them paid a fair, living wage?
                  Is the factory safe?

- **WHO?**   Retailers, consumers.

- **EXPLORE?**   Check labels and online to explore.
                  Ask shop assistants where and how clothes were made.

- **ACTION?**   Consider supporting an initiative like Fashion Revolution.
                  Write to companies asking about their policies.
                  Buy only what you are satified has been fairly produced.

image: fashion revolution

HOW HAVE MY CLOTHES AFFECTED THE ENVIRONMENT?

CARELESS ABUSE or GOOD STEWARDSHIP?

- **ISSUES:** Was an unsustainable amount of the planet's resources used up in the production of my clothing?
  Did the dyes and other chemicals used pollute waterways and endanger human and other life?
  Do the garment washing requirements amplify the problem?
  Can discarded clothes be reused, or will they just go to landfill?

- **WHO?** Retailers, consumers, government, local councils.

- **EXPLORE?** Same as C 1
  Question the sustainability policies of your local council.

- **ACTION?**
  Consider supporting an initiative like Fashion Revolution.
  Write to companies asking about their sustainability policies.
  Buy only what you are satified has been sustainably produced.
  Government and local councils to set an example by focussing investment on sustainable processes and awarding contracts to companies seriously addressing these issues.

THE ONLY THING
NECESSARY FOR THE
TRIUMPH OF EVIL
IS FOR GOOD PEOPLE
TO DO NOTHING

Edmund Burke (adapted)
18th Century Irish statesman

image: fashion revolution

239

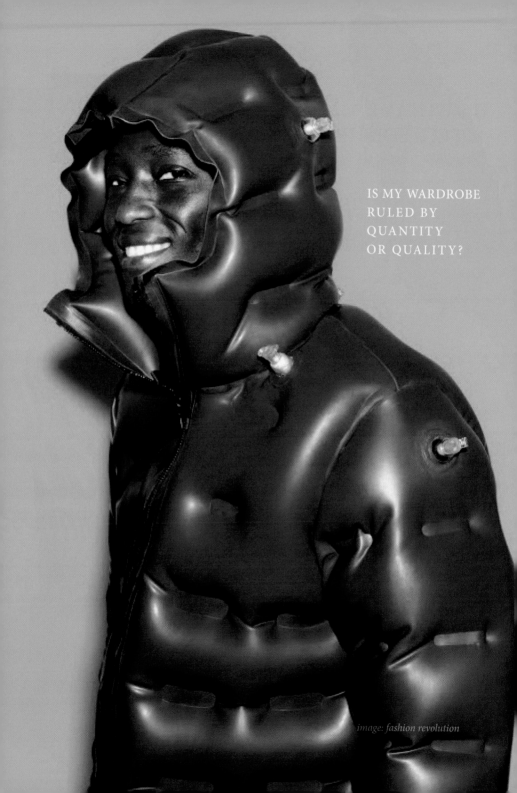

IS MY WARDROBE
RULED BY
QUANTITY
OR QUALITY?

image: fashion revolution

WHAT CLOTHES DO I NEED?

RETAIL THERAPY or THOUGHT OUT WARDROBE?

- ISSUES? How many clothes do I have? Do I need any more?
  Is my wardrobe ruled by quantity or quality?
  Is buying clothes just a recreational pursuit,
     or do I have a real love for what I wear?
  What should I do with clothes I no longer use?

- WHO? Consumers, retailers, advertising agencies, charity sector.

- EXPLORE? Do a wardrobe count - how many tops, shoes etc?
  Ask how many times I have worn each garment?

- ACTION? Consider how I might reduce the size of my wardrobe.
  Check out who might benefit from what I don't need.
  Review my approach to next season's wardrobe.
  Challenge how advertising blindly drives demand,
     regardless of cost and consequence.

CONSUMERS IN THE UK
HAVE AN ESTIMATED
£30 BILLION WORTH OF
UNWORN CLOTHING
IN THEIR WARDROBES

241

c4 DOES THAT SUIT ME?

ILLUSION or REALITY?

- ISSUES?   Does what I wear suit me?
              Do I let fashion imagery distort my view of myself?
              Can stylists and editors use their influence more responsibly,
                  ... yet still embrace their creativity and point of view?

- WHO?   Consumers, websites, stylists, editors.

- EXPLORE?   Go online to gain insight into what colours and looks suit me.
              Consider trying something new ... being more ambitious!
              Look critically at magazine, online and social media imagery.

- ACTION?   Ask friends and shop assistants for honest input.
              Don't be frightened of making mistakes.
              Write to editors challenging unhelpful images.

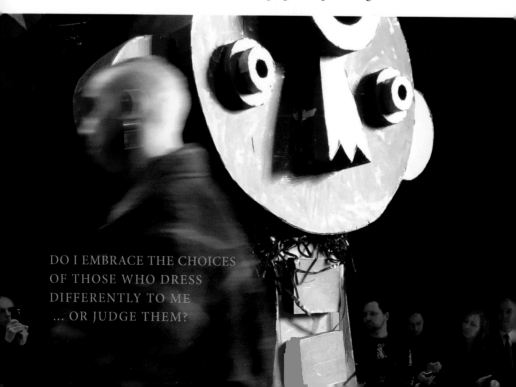

DO I EMBRACE THE CHOICES
OF THOSE WHO DRESS
DIFFERENTLY TO ME
... OR JUDGE THEM?

IS MODESTY OUTDATED?

SELF EXPRESSION or MODEST RESTRAINT?

- ISSUES?   Do I have any responsibility to others for the impact
                    of the way I dress?
                    Do I embrace the choices of those who dress differently
                        to me ... or judge them?
                    Need dressing modestly mean dowdiness?
                    Are restraint and self-expression compatible?
                    Am I denying who I am if I suppress how I like to dress?

- WHO?   Everyone.

- EXPLORE?   How I look makes a big contribution to how others see me
                    ... so it's worth spending time considering this one.

- ACTION?   As this is such a personal choice, I'm not going to comment
                    on the issues raised, other than to invite their consideration
                    and share below a few thoughts (not all are serious!) from
                    the famous.

WHEN YOU'VE GOT IT
FLAUNT IT
Mel Brooks, The Producers

EXPRESS YOURSELF
N. W.A.

MODESTY IS THE
HIGHEST ELEGANCE
Coco Chanel

MODESTY IS ALWAYS
BEAUTIFUL
G K Chesterton

I WANT FREEDOM FOR
THE FULL EXPRESSION
OF MY PERSONALITY
Mahatma Gandhi

I WISH I HAD INVENTED
BLUE JEANS. THEY HAVE
EXPRESSION, MODESTY,
SEX APPEAL, SIMPLICITY:
ALL I HOPE FOR IN MY
CLOTHES
Yves Saint Laurent

WELCOME YOUNG PEOPLE
AND TREAT THEM WELL
- THEY ARE YOUR PRESENT
AS WELL AS YOUR FUTURE

A CAREER IN FASHION?

INDULGENT WASTE or RICH OPPORTUNITY?

- ISSUES?   Is there a career in fashion that fits my skills?
            Does fashion provide opportunities for a good career?
            How do I find the right way in?

- WHO?   Young people, parents, education sector, employers,
               industry bodies.

- EXPLORE? Don't assume the first person spoken to knows what it's all about!
            Go online to British Fashion Council and other reputable
               websites to explore opportunities.
            Consider different options eg: straight into a job, apprenticeship,
               foundation course/BTEC, university degree.

- ACTION?   Explore what it's like - eg. attend a Saturday Club.
            Gain experience where possible - eg. Saturday job in retail.
            Visit events like London Fashion WeekEnd and Clothes Show Live.
            Fashion is not for the faint hearted or lazy! Consider if it's what
               you really want. Don't be easily put off!
            Parents and career advisors - find out facts before advising!
            Employers - welcome young people and treat them well.
               They are your present, as well as your future.

IF YOU HAVE A DREAM DON'T GIVE UP
DON'T LET CIRCUMSTANCES PUT YOU OFF
Daniel Blake, Designer

C7   WHAT PRICE FOR YOUTH?

UNPAID EXPERIENCE or PAID WORK?

- ISSUES? Should interns and other young people be paid?
  Is invaluable experience benefit enough?
  Am I likely to get the best talent if I don't pay?

- WHO? Employers, interns, industry bodies, government.

- EXPLORE? Consider the legal situation. Visit HMRC and other websites.
  Do I see the training of young people as a major opportunity
      or a drain on scarce resources?
  Am I exploiting a young person?
  Am I fussed about social justice?

- ACTION? Employers - give a young person a chance?
  Interns - don't undervalue your worth. Don't be intimidated.
  Industry & HMRC - adapt guidelines to give sufficient flexibility
      between a short term 'taster' and longer term experience.

C8   ALL WORK, NO PLAY?

DRIVEN LABOUR or COMMITTED TEAMWORK?

- ISSUES? What is a good work/life balance for fashion?
  Will regular breaks help me stay healthy, productive ... and creative?

- WHO? Employers, employees, retailers, consumers, government, churches.

- EXPLORE? Employers - have I instilled a long hours mentality?
  Employees - am I feeling increasingly stressed over my work?
  Retailers - has profit become more important than people?
  Consumers - has my freedom of choice become others' work prison?

- ACTION? Employers and employees to review working hours pattern.
  Government to consider long term effect of seven day shop opening.
  Churches to review support for those having to work on Sundays.

EMPLOYERS - GIVE
A YOUNG PERSON
A CHANCE

9 THE CHARACTER OF FASHION

character (n) : distinctive mark

RAG TRADE or CARING PROFESSION?

GOD'S HEART FOR FASHION seems to me to centre not so much around what we do, more how we do it. Individual character and, yes, the character of the industry.

Fashion is a commercial industry, with the complexities of global scale, so it is always going to be a challenge to break out of the accepted norm, which will often reflect long established patterns of practice and decision taking that both companies and individuals feel they have no choice but to make - or go out of business.

Yet, a tag cloud (opposite), showing by size of word the principal perceptions of fashion amongst, I would suggest, the majority, is not something I am proud of. The creativity, passion and plain hard work of those working in fashion and the pride and fun of wearing clothes would be dwarfed by words like brutal, stressful, exploitative ... Is this the best we can do?

Which brings me back to God's Heart #10 (*page 227*), which can give us insight into how God might want to change the world of fashion in this day. We might consider it as a wardrobe from which we dress daily.

I have taken ten character traits from Colossians 3:12-16 (quoted in #10), and suggest which of the issues raised they might apply to and potentially transform, if applied in the day to day. They divide into characteristics for the industry to adopt, and those for the individual. Change will always start with the individual, but must work its way through to the corporate, if it is to have significant and lasting impact.

Together, they might start a transformation of fashion's reputation.

CHANGE WILL ALWAYS START WITH THE INDIVIDUAL
BUT MUST WORK ITS WAY THROUGH TO THE CORPORATE
IF IT IS TO HAVE SIGNIFICANT AND LASTING IMPACT

HARSH

ANXIOUS

GLAMOROUS

FAIR

INDULGENT

WEIRD

HARD WORK

KIND

PRETENTIOUS

FUN

BRUTAL

COLLABORATIVE

EXPLOITATIVE

CARING

POORLY PAID

CREATIVE

INACCESSIBLE

RESPONSIBLE

DAMAGING

OPEN

RELENTLESS

OPPORTUNITY

STRESSFUL

IMPORTANT

NARCISSISTIC

WIDE REACHING

DARK

ADDICTIVE

INSPIRING

IN CROWD

EXHILARATING

JUDGEMENTAL

COMPASSION - *sweat shops, health & safety, fair pay*
LIVE AID, in the 1980s, was a clarion call to awaken the wealthy West to the scale of global need and, with it, compassion. We often hear, today, of 'compassion fatigue'. But this is a luxury we cannot indulge in. A sense of injustice is close to many people's heart, and this needs to apply to everyone. Genuine compassion will move us on from emotion to press for action on such realities as safe factories and fair pay - for all workers in all countries, whether we work in fashion or consume it.

DISCIPLINE - *body image, working hours, pay for young people*
HOW easy not to worry about the effect on others of "what I want." A stylist wants a certain (skinny) look, but doesn't think of, or care about its impact on those viewing the imagery created. "Not my problem." ... "I'm staying up all night to finish what I'm doing, and expect others to do likewise" ... regardless of *their* circumstances. ... "They're benefitting from this work experience more than me - why should I pay them?" ... All valid options, but are they good choices? It takes concern for others to consider the bigger picture, and discipline to implement better choices.

QUIET STRENGTH - *careers, sexuality*
PARENT *to Daughter:* "Is fashion **really** the best career?
We just want the best for you." ... *Employer:* "Dare I risk
taking on an untried youngster?" ... *Christian:* "I don't see
how gay relationships stack up with the Bible, so I'm steering
clear of fashion, as so many gay people seem to work there."
We often try to avoid what we don't understand. It takes
an inner, quiet strength to go with it, regardless. Similarly,
it can take courage to be the person we believe we have been
made to be, even though those around might not 'get it'.

INSTRUCT ONE ANOTHER
- *environment, fast fashion, modest dressing*
RESEARCHING this book, I found out more about the
risks posed to the planet by fashion (fast fashion, in
particular), than I had in over thirty years working in the
industry. Similarly, one interviewee chided me for a
"male chauvanistic" approach to modest dressing which
I was glad to hear, as it gave me a much more balanced
approach. Will we listen to one another? If we will, there
is a good chance that the industry will grow in a more
healthy and sustainable fashion.

INSTRUCT AND DIRECT ONE ANOTHER
USING GOOD COMMON SENSE *Colossians 3:16*

KINDNESS
FASHION has such potential to be enjoyable and life
enhancing, making a highly positive impact on communities.
It seems more than a shame, then, that so many are dubious
of it - particularly, as I have discovered, in the cloisters
of the church. Whereas the previous character traits all
challenge what I would describe as poor approaches,
kindness can be the key to unlock the huge reservoir
of energy, great ideas and good will that I have found
throughout the world of fashion. See the example of
Style for Soldiers. To release this wonderful gift, however,
requires the personal attributes we now move on to consider.

CHARACTER OF THE INDIVIDUAL

HUMILITY, FORGIVE, EVEN TEMPERED

THERE'S an awful lot of attitude in fashion. Feathers can fly when things are not going well. Gossip abounds. Is it surprising, therefore, that it can be an uncomfortable place to work? Is it surprising that wary parents might be reluctant to see their offspring entering this world? Such attitude is self perpetuating, but it needn't be so. A little bit of humility goes a long way. It is simply a realistic assessment of ourselves. It can take the wind out of unwarranted attitude, temper tantrums, and open eyes in realisation that a finger pointed has three fingers pointing back at myself. It doesn't reduce everyone and everything to a lowest common denominator, rather, it recognises and applauds true talent for what it is.

CONTENT WITH SECOND PLACE

FOLLOWING humility, comes the honest and realistic assessment that we need and should be grateful for leaders, but accept that not everyone is a leader. I've been no. 2 for much of my working life. And this applies not just to leadership, but to wider roles. I have sat on many interview panels, where it has been clear that the skills of the student being interviewed lie in a supporting role, for example as a pattern cutter, yet so often the advice has fallen on deaf ears. Does the interviewee want what they see as fulfilment ... and glory? For most, it will lead to disillusionment, as they have to settle for what they see as second best. Yet, second place and second best are very different things. Ladder climbing is exhausting and, ultimately, pointless. Discovering and developing our gifts is what we were made for.

THANKFULNESS

THIS leads us to thankfulness. Thankfulness for who we are, the gifts we have been blessed with, the opportunities that have come our way. Please note, there's a big difference between thankfulness and being satified. Both the creative and administrative side of me are always pushing to be better, to discover new ways of doing things ... and, in my case, seeking to discover God's unfolding plans for my life. So I am often dissatisfied. But I can always be thankful for what I have and where I am.

PEACE

WITH thankfulness comes peace. An inner peace that goes deeper than how I feel, and the ability to overcome temporary dissatisfaction with how things are going at any particular time. For many years, I had a Bible verse written on a piece of card on my desk. It said this: *Do not be anxious about anything but in everything, by prayer and petition with thanksgiving, present your requests to God. And the peace of God, which passes understanding, will guard your hearts and minds in Christ Jesus Philippians 4:6,7*

LOVE

FINALLY, if we know peace, we are set free to cease worrying so much about ourselves and what we are doing, and to look outwards to those around us who need help, support, opportunity, justice. This is love, where love is treating others as we would wish to be treated ourselves. It is not something we feel; it is something we choose. Like what we wear.

... FULL CIRCLE ...

WHICH brings us full circle. We have seen snapshots of an industry, gained insights into lives spent working in it, been challenged by some of the issues it faces, had a sneak preview of how God might perceive it.

When all is said and done, fashion is about the people working in it, and those engaging with it from many different perspectives. The way the industry works and how it is perceived, its reputation, is entirely in our hands. To eradicate the bad and build on the good takes individual decisions. And the decisions we take gradually build our character.

What will fashion's character be in the years to come? We will find out from its reputation.

WHATEVER ELSE YOU PUT ON, WEAR LOVE
IT'S YOUR BASIC ALL-PURPOSE GARMENT
Colossians 3:14

CHARACTER IS LIKE A TREE
AND REPUTATION LIKE A
SHADOW. THE SHADOW IS
WHAT WE THINK OF IT; THE
TREE IS THE REAL THING
Abraham Lincoln

255

I HAVE A DREAM ...

INSPIRED BY DR MARTIN LUTHER KING, JR

I HAVE A DREAM ... where those working in fashion look into the mirror and allow their gaze to carry beyond how well they like what they see, to reflect on the impact of what they do, and how they do it.

I HAVE A DREAM ... where those of us who enjoy wearing fashion, wake up to what we are buying into, think through its implications, and choose our clothes with care.

I HAVE A DREAM ... where opportunity, fulfilment and blessing are enjoyed by those involved through all fashion's processes: from cotton fields to catwalk, sampling room to shopping mall, design studio to dance floor

I HAVE A DREAM ... of a new generation stepping forward with the determination and confidence to do things differently.

I HAVE A DREAM ... where fashion, renowned for its creativity and hard work, becomes as well known for its care and kindness.

I HAVE A DREAM ... of diverse, energetic and talented people increasingly trusted to use responsibly their great capacity to influence.

I HAVE A DREAM ... of a mighty industry holding its head up high with pride, as it sees its immense power being transformed into a global force for the good of all.

THIS IS MY HOPE ...

10 TEN PRAYERS FOR FASHION

MANY people pray - even if the words differ and the recipient varies.

This book has sought to weave together specifically Christian perspectives with those of experts in the world of fashion. Many I have spoken to have been sympathetic to this fusion, even if they might not share my Christian faith.

Suggested prayers have been dropped in throughout the book, but it seemed right to conclude with ten prayers for fashion - for those who work in it, teach it, make it, write about it ... and those who consume it, which is all of us.

A word of encouragement: you don't need to be an expert to pray; God hears the cry of our hearts as clearly as spoken prayer. Similarly, we don't need to wait until we are in a group (eg. in a church), before we pray. There is nowhere better than being in the thick of it to send a brief prayer upwards, asking God to help us as we tackle our day to day challenges.

The stories and issues I have shared reveal an industry rich in opportunity, but also shot through with challenges, practical and ethical.

On our own, we might make a few dents in some of these. But if we want to see definitive and long term change for the better, my belief is that it is the power of prayer, releasing the willing hand of God, that will make the difference. Such was the power, in past centuries, that helped set up the first schools and hospitals, and saw through the abolition of the slave trade.

I invite you to join me in praying that fashion, so often the object of criticism, might become a leading global force for the good of all in the 21st Century.

LORD, MAKE ME AN INSTRUMENT OF THY PEACE.
WHERE THERE IS HATRED, LET ME SOW LOVE,
WHERE THERE IS INJURY, PARDON;
WHERE THERE IS DOUBT, FAITH;
WHERE THERE IS DESPAIR, HOPE;
WHERE THERE IS DARKNESS, LIGHT;
AND WHERE THERE IS SADNESS, JOY
O DIVINE MASTER, GRANT THAT I MAY NOT SO MUCH SEEK
TO BE CONSOLED AS TO CONSOLE,
TO BE UNDERSTOOD AS TO UNDERSTAND,
TO BE LOVED, AS TO LOVE
FOR IT IS IN GIVING THAT WE RECEIVE,
IT IS IN PARDONING THAT WE ARE PARDONED,
AND IT IS IN DYING THAT WE ARE BORN TO ETERNAL LIFE

Francis of Assisi

THE MORE YOU PRAY
THE LESS YOU'LL PANIC

Rick Warren

I HAVE SO MUCH TO DO THAT I
SHALL SPEND THE FIRST THREE
HOURS IN PRAYER

Martin Luther

I HAVE BEEN DRIVEN MANY
TIMES UPON MY KNEES BY
THE OVERWHELMING
CONVICTION THAT I HAD
NOWHERE ELSE TO GO. MY
OWN WISDOM AND THAT
OF ALL ABOUT ME SEEMED
INSUFFICIENT FOR THAT DAY

Abraham Lincoln

PRAYER IS NOT ASKING. IT IS
A LONGING OF THE SOUL. IT
IS DAILY ADMISSION OF ONE'S
WEAKNESS. IT IS BETTER IN
PRAYER TO HAVE A HEART
WITHOUT WORDS THAN WORDS
WITHOUT A HEART

Mahatma Gandhi

IS PRAYER YOUR STEERING WHEEL
OR YOUR SPARE TYRE? *Corrie ten Boom*

LET US PRAY

PRAY WITHOUT CEASING
1 Thessalonians 5:17 New King James Version

FATHER GOD, inspire those working in fashion to use their talents to the full; to welcome those who have a different vision; to put people before profit; to show kindness to one another - that the world might look on, and see that this is an industry that cares. AMEN

+1 INDUSTRY

FATHER GOD, open the eyes of consumers to the impact of their purchases on the sustainability of the planet and the fairness of reward paid to those who have made the clothes. Show people which clothes reveal their true personality, and which lead them to try and be someone they are not. AMEN

+2 CONSUMERS

FATHER GOD, direct Ministers and their teams to recognise and support the particular needs of fashion and the creative industries: that apprenticeships might be protected, colleges and universities developed in a way that is fit for purpose; and guidance and legislation to protect workers, consumers and the environment, be meaningful and effective. AMEN

+3 GOVERNMENT

FATHER GOD, inspire those who teach fashion to reveal in young people the creativity You have gifted them. Release, in a new generation, the confidence to express themselves fearlessly yet, with respect for the effect they have on all who are impacted by their designs and the way they are presented. AMEN

+4 EDUCATION

FATHER GOD, empower those seeking to change attitudes amongst parents and careers advisors, to see that fashion can be an inspiring career choice for those with the right talent. Open the eyes of the fashion industry to see the potential of young people, that it might invest in them. AMEN

+5 CAREERS

FATHER GOD, breathe fresh understanding into church leaders, that they might gain greater insight into their congregations' places of work, offering encouragement and support, not just to their own members but, through them, to all those they work with - that their workplaces, and the people around them, might experience transformation for the good. AMEN

+6 CHURCHES

FATHER GOD, strengthen all those who are doing something positive to address where fashion gets it wrong. Enable Fashion Revolution and similar initiatives, to make a real difference to the lives of millions around the world, and to the sustainability of the planet. AMEN

+7 CAMPAIGNS

FATHER GOD, grant wisdom, honesty, clarity and sensitivity to journalists, bloggers, editors and PRs working in fashion. Guide them to investigate and write with insight and integrity, committed to revealing truth, but also seeking to be part of the solution to challenges and not simply creating headlines. AMEN

+8 MEDIA

STRENGTHEN THOSE WHO WORK FOR SUSTAINABILITY, FAIRNESS, RESTRAINT AND SENSITIVE RESPONSIBILITY

FATHER GOD, help those who name You as Saviour and Lord, to be strong salt and bright light in the workplace: that their colleagues might see their motives are good, their work, excellent, their patience, steadfast, and their love for all they work with, constant. May groups like Fashion for Christ and gModa be not just an oasis for Christians, but a place where all those working in fashion are prayed for and supported. AMEN

+9 CHRISTIANS IN FASHION

THEIR MOTIVES, GOOD
THEIR WORK, EXCELLENT
THEIR PATIENCE, STEADFAST
THEIR LOVE FOR ALL THEY
WORK WITH, CONSTANT

FATHER GOD, the fashion industry has the scale and power to exploit the planet, workers and consumers alike. Stay the hand of those who would blindly seek to maximise profit, and strengthen those who work for sustainability, fairness, restraint and sensitive responsibility - that fashion might come to be seen as a global force for the good of all. AMEN

+10 GLOBAL FORCE FOR GOOD

STRONG SALT AND BRIGHT
LIGHT IN THE WORKPLACE

THE PRAYER OF A RIGHTEOUS PERSON
IS POWERFUL AND EFFECTIVE

James 5:16

commandment #10
FASHION TO BE SEEN
AS A GLOBAL FORCE
FOR THE GOOD OF ALL